REDBACK 7

Other books in the Redbacks series:

Battlers and Billionaires:
The Story of Inequality in Australia
ANDREW LEIGH

Why We Argue about Climate Change
ERIC KNIGHT

Dog Days: Australia after the Boom
ROSS GARNAUT

Anzac's Long Shadow: The Cost of Our National Obsession
JAMES BROWN

Crime & Punishment: Offenders and Victims
in a Broken Justice System
RUSSELL MARKS

Supermarket Monsters: The Price of Coles
and Woolworths' Dominance
MALCOLM KNOX

www.blackincbooks.com

AN ECONOMY IS NOT A SOCIETY

WINNERS AND LOSERS IN
THE NEW AUSTRALIA

Dennis Glover

Published by Redback,
an imprint of Schwartz Publishing Pty Ltd
37–39 Langridge Street
Collingwood VIC 3066 Australia
enquiries@blackincbooks.com
www.blackincbooks.com

The National Library of Australia Cataloguing-in-Publication entry:

    Glover, Dennis, 1964– author.
    An economy is not a society: winners and losers in the new
    Australia / Dennis Glover.
    9781863957472 (paperback)
    9781925203363 (ebook)
    Economic development—Australia. Government
    productivity—Australia. Australia—Economic policy.
    Australia—Politics and government—History.
    338.994

Cover design by Peter Long
Cover photograph by Roger Howard
Photographs on pages 15, 20 and 23 by Wolfgang Sievers; used with
permission of the Pictures Collection, State Library of Victoria

CONTENTS

To Toby and Teddy,
just so you know where you're coming from.

It is not now as it hath been of yore;—
Turn wheresoe'ere I may,
By night or day,
The things which I have seen I now can see no more.
—WILLIAM WORDSWORTH

DARK VISION

Thirty years ago, Australia's self-styled economic reformers began a revolution that
they won and the little people lost. This revolution devastated numerous once affluent
working-class communities like the one in
which I grew up, turning many of their inhabitants into
something entirely new: the non-working class. Like all
revolutions, it produced a grand reform narrative that
portrays its leaders as heroes and those who oppose them
as naive and self-interested reactionaries. This one-sided
narrative must now be challenged.

At the heart of this tired revolution – which lurches
along, led by the managerialist class it placed in power –
is Joseph Schumpeter's concept of 'creative destruction':
the idea that in order to create a new economy, we must

continually annihilate the old one. The task now is to rid ourselves of this heartless and morally barren concept and rediscover our moral voice so we can build a country that is once again worthy of us.

When you think about it, creative destruction is an ingenious piece of doublethink. By smashing things up, it claims, we are actually building them, and the people whose little world is being smashed should thank us for doing such a good job of it. The demolitionist becomes the engineer, the economist becomes the hero, the pig stands on two legs. But, we should ask, can an economic theory exist in the absence of a moral position? And if it can't, what is the moral position of creative destruction?

In an aside in his famous history of the great economists, *The Worldly Philosophers*, Robert L. Heilbroner – who studied under Schumpeter at Harvard – gives us a clue. He tells us that in the late 1930s, after the Wall Street Crash had delivered power to the Nazis and created the preconditions for World War II, Schumpeter's students were regularly shocked to hear him 'declare, with obvious enjoyment, that depressions, far from being unmitigated social evils, were actually in the nature of "a good cold douche" for the economic system!' The Great Depression a *good* thing? The inventor of creative destruction seems to have had all the morality of a pyromaniac.

The idea of creative destruction is presented to us as reason itself, and far superior to the romantic nostalgia of those who protest against it. But is creative destruction really better? Is it based purely on reason? Or is it motivated by a dark vision of humanity? Does it have its own bleak – or, more accurately, shallow and banal – conception of life and how it should be lived? Let's find out. Let's investigate the economic reformers' idea of creative destruction from the point of view of some of those on the receiving end.

Where should we start? At home.

When Australian economists turn to economic reform, something strange happens: they reflexively start talking about China, the way a man cheating on his wife can't help but mention his mistress. 'Look at this aerial photograph of modern Shanghai,' they say. 'Look at it glitter, look at it gleam! There, in China – that's our future, and creative destruction will help us reach it.' I want them to talk about Australia for a change – not just the bits they can see from their business-class window seats as they depart for the cities of Asia, or the abstractions represented on their PowerPoint slides. Specifically, I want them to talk about the places where a lot of the destruction took place, like my old home town, whose fate, sadly, is not unique.

Once they do, something becomes obvious: not everyone is a winner from economic reform. Their friend creative destruction may indeed create, but it also destroys – usually the lives of other people in far-off suburbs, about whom they know little and care less; people who don't have access to the opinion pages of the national dailies to tell us how well it's all working out, now that the factories are gone and the unions have been broken and the public assets have been sold off and the middle classes with their private schools and private hospitals have cut free and left. These are people for whom Australia hasn't necessarily changed for the better.

So let's change our focus. Let's put away the wide-angle camera lens, walk through some back streets, disobey the 'Do Not Enter' signs and have a good look at the results of the revolution the economic reformers began thirty years ago. If the creative destroyers want to take credit for all that glitters and all that gleams, then they must also take the blame for all the broken glass and all the graffiti and all the rust and all the pop-up rubbish dumps that now pollute our vision.

This is the story of what the creative destroyers have done. It is the story of a revolution that the little people lost.

CHAPTER 1
PLACES OF THE HEART

Sous les pavés, la plage!
—Street graffiti, Paris, 1968

You may not have heard of Doveton. Many people haven't, including some who have lived in Melbourne their whole lives. Doveton is down the Princes Highway and the Monash Freeway, just beyond Dandenong, about thirty-five kilometres south-east of the CBD. It was once a far more prosperous place – never wealthy, but a place where cars and trucks and trains and diesel engines and refrigerators and processed food were made; where mums and dads alike had decent-paying jobs; where the schools sent smart children to university even before university education became ubiquitous; where the streets were neat and tidy and the shopping strips pleasant; and where the working class enjoyed perhaps its greatest level of relative prosperity since economic history first began.

That's how I remember it, anyway, because Doveton is where I grew up. I know what some are going to say – 'I'll bet he doesn't live there now' – and they'd be right. Like most from my generation in Doveton, I moved out after going to university. But my family remains in the area and remains working-class, my friends from my Doveton days are still my friends, I travel there all the time, and like many others who grew up there, my heart has never left. But enough of that. I want to start by going back in time and talking about my little world, the world before the revolution, and the people who once lived in it. Let's go back to my neighbourhood. As places go, it may not seem that extraordinary, but in an essential way its fate explains what has changed in our country and even within our-selves. Perhaps you know somewhere just like it.

It's 1975, I'm eleven years old and I'm playing cricket in the middle of my crescent. The nature strips are a four, and it's a six if you can hit it over the front fence of anyone's house. There's no risk of getting in trouble, as everyone's dads are at work.

On the off side, number 28's dad works at Perkin's Engines, number 30's (my dad) is at General Motors Holden, and so is 32's – he's a GMH line manager and the owner of a flashy Chrysler Charger, which our eyes follow every time it comes down the street. From memory, 34 and 36 were in vehicle production too, probably at Inter-national Harvester. On the on side, 27 works for Ford (I think it must have been in retail, as the Ford plants were far away), 29 is a self-employed car mechanic, and 31 is an engineer called Boothroyd – the only person in our street with a university degree; he works on the Holden design staff and is an officer in dad's Dandenong-based Army Reserve artillery battery.

My best friends, two of the players in our games of street cricket, were John Pandazopoulos ('Panda', naturally, who later became a left-wing Labor MP in the Victorian parliament) and Jimmy (later 'Jim', who would work his way up from apprentice draughtsman to a management role in a major manufacturing company). Panda's dad worked as a cleaner in the same GMH plant as mine, and Jimmy's dad ran a small garage that specialised in converting imported American cars from left-hand to right-hand drive; every week there'd be a wonderful new Chevy or Ford or Chrysler sitting in his front drive, and we often got to have joyrides in them. Later, when we turned eighteen, we drove them to local pubs on Friday and Saturday nights.

Cars – their design, manufacture, repair and sale – gave us our bread and butter, our political direction and our social structure. They were the art we created and the delight of our little community, which centred on the primary school and neat strip shopping centre just beyond the end of the crescent, with its kindergarten and its stop for the bus that would take us to the big department stores and cinemas in Dandenong. Our mothers worked too, in little shops and in Coles and on the line in the canning and clothing factories not far away. Compared to our grandparents' lives, ours were unbelievably affluent. We hadn't had to survive the Blitz or get torpedoed on the Atlantic. And, knowing nothing better, we couldn't have wanted for more.

I'm sure you get the picture: my little valley was green, and made greener by the fallibility of memory. But even after adding in the imperfections, here was a community built for us little people, in the age before capital cut itself free from our democratic control. In it were factory managers, factory workers, small-business people, teachers and even the odd professional, all living together and sending their children to school together. No wonder our dads were in the Army Reserve: this was worth fighting for.

It all added up to something that worked. But take the car and truck and canning factories and the nice shops out of this equation, and you'd have lost more than simply jobs: you'd be commencing a risky social experiment that only the most sophisticated and forward-thinking societies could have made into a success. But forty years ago, that was all in the future.

Something keeps drawing me back to the crescent. A few years ago, when Dad died, I stood outside my old house and wept, but not just for him. No more fours and sixes to hit here – the fences are long gone, and the nature strips and front yards are buried under concrete and rusting cars, with only the odd weed reaching instinctively for the sunshine. The house next to mine had a dirty caravan out the front, just visible behind a collection of abandoned vehicles and miscellaneous junk, and the one opposite looked similarly forlorn. What made me shudder, though, was the sight of my own former home, where I lived until I went to university just after my eighteenth birthday in 1982. Its collection of tow-trucks, decaying vehicles and stacks of metal panelling were suggestive of a junkyard – and in fact I later discovered that it was advertised on numerous online commercial listings as just that: a commercial wrecking yard and automotive spare parts business.

While it was unsightly in the extreme, I had to admit to a certain amount of respect for the new owners, who, after the collapse of the car industry, were at least managing to keep it alive in some way. The managers in Detroit and the economic commentators in Sydney and Canberra don't love cars anymore, but these people did and one had to admire that. But it told you something else too: that the occupiers of my little house had gone from builders to wreckers, from manufacturers to spare parts sellers, from craftsmen to gleaners in just one generation: here is the economic progress we were told would make us all wealthier, now acting in reverse. When did it all start to go wrong? When the factories started closing down.

In the Doveton of my memories it is permanent summer; more precisely, it is permanent Christmas. Because our parents worked at both the General Motors Holden plant (Dad) and the Heinz canning factory (Mum), my sisters and I were among the luckiest kids in town. We had not one but two factory incomes, which was enough back then for us to be among the affluent working class. More importantly, it meant we got to go the children's Christmas parties run by the social clubs at both factories.

There is an image of that time stamped indelibly on my memory. Back in the mid-1960s GMH had commissioned an artist to produce an advertisement for its latest EH model station wagon. It was the sort of futuristic vision you could imagine Salvatore in the art department of Sterling Cooper coming up with in an early series of *Mad Men*: a shiny new car, its chromed bumper bar, mirrors and other fittings gleaming in the sunshine as it whooshed down the highway, with father at the wheel, mother beside him in chic sunglasses and 2.5 children in the back, smiling at their schoolmates being left behind in the car's wake. This was the future, and we were already living in it! I saw an image of the ad recently in a history of Holden cars.

The Christmas parties themselves were everything a child could dream of, with showground rides, ponies, mini-bikes, concerts and a present that was really worth having. One year, Santa arrived in a helicopter. These were lavish affairs, paid for by the companies but organised by the workers themselves, although there was likely not a single university graduate or professional event planner among them. Here is a little world lost – one the workers controlled in a way almost impossible to imagine now.

Today, when we think of trade unions, what first comes to mind are the massive industry superannuation funds that the union leaders now control. This is in some ways an advance: as Marx would surely have noted, it means the workers have at last got control of a good proportion of the nation's capital (which is, of course, why the industry super funds are in the Liberal Party's sights). But it hides a major loss, one probably not worth the gain of all that finance, with all its tempting corruptions for the average union official. Gone is a culture and a movement, an autonomous, self-organised community with its own cohesion, living in part by its own rules and to its own rhythms, looking after its own. Gone is a time when working-class Australians controlled some of their own turf; when their unions controlled knock-off time; when holidays came in annual cycles and everyone actually got holiday pay; when overtime would pay for a new car or a new kitchen or a treat for the kids; when their shops closed for the evenings and most of the weekend and the retail lobbies didn't complain about paying penalty rates; when life for many wasn't reduced to a state of constant exhaustion by casual, deregulated work; when people could enjoy the festive season without being dog-tired from the Christmas Eve nightshift, and stressed out by the prospect of an early start to the Boxing Day sales. Gone is a time when life, in many easily definable ways, for a great many people, truly was better.

The historian views the world differently, forever stripping back decades of paint and renovations with a kind of compulsion to see what lies beneath. I can never, for example, walk around London without every line of the ugly post-war buildings conjuring the Tudor or Georgian architecture that stood there before the Luftwaffe destroyed it in the Blitz – finer, more beautiful, more human. *Sous les pavés, la plage! Under the cobblestones, the beach! Under the ugliness, a better life!*

A couple of examples in particular come to mind. While I was studying at Cambridge, my supervisor took me to what had been until recently a little-thought-of storage area up in the roof of his college. The removal of a false ceiling and the stripping of paint had revealed it for what it really was: a magnificent medieval reading library with a tall, oak-beamed ceiling like the hull of an upturned sailing ship. It had all been 'modernised' less than a lifetime before, but the memory of the original had not been passed on to succeeding generations of dons and so had been forgotten. On another occasion, a friend called Andy, an expert in pre-modern economic history, took me for drinks to an underground bar in Norwich – a rough, mean-looking place with over-loud music – to show me how it had originally been a warehouse servicing the late-medieval English wool trade. It was nothing more than a bricked cellar, in no way spectacular, but to the historian it was evidence of a way of life that had been smashed to pieces by the steam-powered loom and the coming of capitalism. Look closely, and you can find vanished worlds. *Sous les pavés, la plage!* In Australia, lacking in grand ancient architecture, this isn't so easy – unless, of course, you know where to look.

The giant factories used to be like little walled cities: their long fencelines stretching for miles around their borders, broken only by a gatehouse, past which thousands of cars would stream every morning to an overflowing factory car park. In the centre of the complex a giant building housing the boilers that provided the heat and compressed air would sound the siren for the start of each working day. The employees, having already clocked on with their punch cards and now waiting at their stations, would hear the clanking of cans as a conveyor belt came to life, or see the naked chassis of a sedan begin its journey along an assembly line, from which, four hours later, a finished car would emerge, to be driven off to another enormous parking lot. You couldn't miss the old factories then, but today you just might.

The entrance to the old General Motors Holden factory in Dandenong is now a public road, 'Assembly Drive'; half-finished and unsealed in places, it looks like the last street in a country town. The vast flat stretches of tarmac, which thousands of gleaming new vehicles once covered, are now empty, weeds growing though cracks. I spot an old rusting truck, abandoned by the plant's former owners; long weeds are growing up through its axles, dragging it back into the ground like the tentacles of a giant octopus. On the space's north-eastern edge, the concrete shell of a prefabricated shopping centre rises from the dust of passing trucks, proclaiming unsubtly what the future holds: shopping for products made by some cowed but energetic proletariat in China.

There are a few more signs of life. At the complex's westernmost edge, the neatly landscaped headquarters of the Holden Service Parts Operations (HSPO) division looks out over what once was, much in the way a once great country house, now forced to let in tourists to pay for repairs to its leaking roof, looks down on the village over which it used to rule. If you look at the aerial photograph of the place on Google Maps and compare it to the photographs taken from aeroplanes when the plant was in its pomp, you can make out the path of the original roads, the foundations of the now demolished guardhouse and the places where swarming assembly lines once stood. They are now in the process of being replaced by warehouses of bolted concrete and steel sheeting. Since the Google shots were taken a few years back, even more of the old factory buildings have disappeared. This, you imagine, is how archaeologists reconstruct the sites of former Greek settlements along the Mediterranean – the long shadows at morning and sunset revealing the sites of razed markets and temples, the retreat of the sea showing a once thriving Phoenician port.

At the end of the road you come across a rental storage yard for the sort of prefabricated huts that construction firms hire out to building sites as places for labourers and engineers to have their morning tea – a sort of disposable slum of the industrial era, of which not a trace will remain for anyone to memorialise fifty years from now. It's here that you take a left-turn to find the past.

You couldn't miss the factories . . .

I've travelled back to the site with Panda. After finishing school, we both went to Monash University, joining the Labor Party on the same day back in March 1982 (actually, I joined the Socialist Workers Party first but lasted just a couple of days). We've remained close ever since, although our paths diverged when we were in our mid-twenties: he became the local mayor and then a state MP and minister, while I went off to Cambridge.

At GMH, our dads were both probably representative of the factory workforce in its glory days: my father as a semi-skilled operative drawn to Australia by the promise of something better than could be found in the industrial cities of the United Kingdom, and Panda's as an unskilled peasant from southern Europe escaping from the poverty of a declining village and the oppressive rule of the colonels.

The factory life was in my father's blood. Like his brothers and friends, at age fourteen he had been apprenticed into the Hilden Mill in Lisburn, not far from Belfast. Built in the late 1700s, the mill was one of the very first steam-powered cotton manufactories, and the sort of workplace Friedrich Engels wrote about in *The Condition of the Working Class in England*. Having employed 2000 workers at its height, it closed in 2006; its ancient, gutted facade is now earmarked for an apartment development (which itself has been stalled since the global financial crisis took down the Irish housing construction industry). Dad described the mill, as it was in the early 1960s, as the sort of factory Charles Dickens would have recognised, with massive stationary engines driving spinning machinery via huge wheels and leather belts. His job as a hackle pin setter (a comparatively skilled occupation) was to repair the spinning machines in order to keep the production of linen fabric and high-grade sewing thread running efficiently. Dad's grandfather had been a labourer at Harland and Wolff shipyards, bashing thousands of infamously brittle rivets into the steel hull of the *Titanic* and its sister ships from the White Star Line.

This inheritance of industrial skills made my father

valuable when he migrated to Australia in 1963, and gave him a free pick of available jobs. He'd started at the International Harvester truck assembly plant just down the highway, but soon moved to GMH, where the pay was better, and he remained there for most of the rest of his working life. Such were the people who built our country. Little did they know they were living out the final days of an industrial revolution that had lasted two centuries, until the factory smashers came.

Of the once mighty factory, just a few original buildings with their saw-toothed roofs remain. It's hard for Panda and me to make out exactly what used to be what, with little more than vague memories of factory Christmas parties to go by, so I return a few weeks later with Ian McCleave, a former engineer who became one of Holden Australia's most senior executives, and Russel Nainie, who rose from the factory floor to be one of the company's senior engineers. What remains isn't the old car assembly line but the former HSPO buildings and those that once housed the maintenance and tooling operations. We put on some fluoro vests and hard hats I'd borrowed from a friend who runs a small refrigeration factory in Spotswood and walked in.

It's a strange sensation, re-entering the past to find it echoing and empty. The main feature of the place is the serrated roof, the verticals containing giant windows like those of ancient cathedrals to let in the maximum amount of natural light. This, combined with the vast floor area, gives you the sensation of entering a roofed football stadium on non-game day or a hangar for jumbo jets that have already flown away. Apart from some shelving units at one end, it's completely empty. We continue our walk-through, pointing our outstretched arms here and there, trying to look like engineers on a plant inspection visit, and no one questions us.

As we look around, Russel tells me that under that one roof once worked at least 500 people, but during our tour I could see just five, and I think I may have double-counted at least one of them. It's part of some retail distribution operation, but there doesn't seem to be much going on. It's obvious why there's no security – there's really not much worth stealing, except for a boxed flat-screen TV and a few cheap-looking suits hanging from a wheeled clothes rack that looks like it's been forgotten.

On my earlier visit with Panda, we had crossed over to the other side of the building, which was joined to the spare parts operation by a covered driveway complex. It's here John thinks his dad might once have worked, pushing his broom back and forth down the aisles, smoking the innumerable cigarettes that failed to kill him until he reached ninety-one. We'd managed to find a storeman, who was sympathetic to our story about wanting to tell the plant's history but who – regulations being what they are – couldn't let us in because there were forklift vehicles at work somewhere. When Panda asked him what they were storing, he told us it was sacks of plastic pellets for use in plastic moulding, but he didn't know who used them and what they made. We thanked him and peeked inside to take some photos, which he allowed us to do from behind a chain.

It all had the sort of sad, impermanent air of a place not being used for its intended purpose. When one thinks about the investment that went into the plant's creation, and its fit-out with once edgy industrial technology – much of it paid for by the nation through its subsidies and protection – you can't but feel an immense sense of pathos at how it has all ended up. What a waste. John and I walked through its cavernous remains like visitors through the sacked ruins of Rome. The almost infinite emptiness and solitude begged the question: where had all the jobs gone?

Where have all the jobs gone?

Ian and Russel take me on a walk around the site to look at what remains from its heyday. You can see it on this aerial photograph from 1970:

GMH, an archaeologist's dream ...

Three smaller buildings, now used for warehousing, are all that stands from that time, along with the administration offices at the front of the old canteen. The then modernist structure, built in the late 1950s or early '60s, has been re-clad in glass and metal to bring it up to date; needless to say, this has ruined it completely. So many people had worked there – 5000 at one point – that the old canteen had staged three lunch sittings during the day shift alone. There was also a bank branch, a fishing club, a bowling club, a tennis club and a cricket club; the courts, greens and pitches were kept up by the factory's very own curator. I must have played cricket there as a sixteen-year-old.

No fewer than ten tea ladies were employed to roam the factory floors for elevenses and afternoon tea, which, until some time in the 1980s, was provided free to all employees. When the tea ladies were sacked, coffee vending machines with small plastic cups were installed and a dollar was added to everyone's weekly pay packet to cover the expense – one of the easy Tier 1 trade-offs during one of the innumerable accord agreements of those days. It's a small detail, but crucial when you think about it. If the past was so much poorer than the present, how could they have afforded to give factory workers a cup of tea then but not now?

This strikes me as an argument with a much wider application: according to the economic reformers, we can't afford Medicare or the aged pension anymore either, even though they assure us that the reforms of the 1980s and '90s have made us richer than ever. What alchemy of wealth creation meant that those tea ladies had to join the dole queue, and that an enjoyable part of thousands of people's lives had to be cheapened and ruined? Why do we consider what replaced that past to be somehow superior, and why do we consider the past itself to be something to snigger and scoff at? These are good questions, which our managerialist friends and their boosters in the press would no doubt dismiss with the inadequate word 'efficiency', before themselves contemplating the client-funded cocktail party and dinner on offer that evening after work.

When I recall my father's addiction to tea – which he would drink while still in his blue overalls at the kitchen table each afternoon after work, strong and stewed in his old metal teapot – I imagine how much he must have looked forward to the tea ladies' visits. Real tea! I'm suddenly touched by the thought of him, conscientious, hardworking, never offshoring his tax or turning his wage into a capital gain, putting down his clipboard and leaving his station for a hard-earned break, a difficult and rare smile breaking out over his face as he reaches out and says, 'White, one sugar.' A lifter, enjoying a simple pleasure no longer available to the little people. What sort of person would take that away? An economic reformer, obviously.

Dominating this whole site today is something that is no longer there. The heart of any auto factory isn't its spare parts warehouse or even the tooling workshops with their lathes, skilled toolmakers and apprentices – it is the assembly line. Ian and Russel point me to where it used to stand. The building looks far too modern. Russel tells me that it's been re-roofed and is now the Australian headquarters of HSPO, or at least what's left of it for the foreseeable future, Holden having already announced that it will be ceasing domestic production in 2017. I spy the high fences and the manned guardhouse and quickly conclude that there is absolutely no chance I can bluff my way in, even if I put on my hardhat and carry my clipboard. But where there's a will, there's a way.

A couple of weeks later I'm driving in, past the friendly and busy guard, to my appointment with Barry Crees, manager of the HSPO complex. Ian has sorted it out for me. While I wait for Barry, I notice that in the space of just a fortnight the construction opposite, which had been rising out of the old truck assembly plant, has gone from a metal frame to a roofed and almost fully walled building; as I watch, a crane lowers on another giant concrete panel.

(By the time I leave the plant an hour later, the panel had already been bolted on to form a wall.) How many people will work in this warehouse, I ask myself. Building it has given a team of men work for a few months, but then what? Probably another building, and then another after that. If rapidly throwing up almost empty structures in a building boom is the only source of new jobs, then our economy and job market have become a sort of Ponzi scheme, where building after building needs to be constructed to keep us all one step ahead of the crash.

As we walk through to the warehouse, Barry tells me that the car assembly line plant has in fact been replaced completely. My heart sinks. I thought I'd be wandering across the original factory floor as it twisted around like a large intestine under the framework of the old aerial assembly line, going past the station where my dad worked fitting doors onto cars for almost thirty years.

The jobs of our fathers . . .

Instead, Barry stops me and points to a shallow drain running through rough concrete across a vast open space that is now used as a car park. This was once the floor under the assembly line roof, which stretched far and wide around us, the same area as three Melbourne Cricket Grounds. As shrines go, it's not much, but then most shrines are essentially about the dead things that lie under the ground, and it was enough to rouse in me at least a smidgen of emotion.

A few years earlier I had walked seven miles in the driving autumn rain across the Scottish island of Jura to find the farmhouse in which the dying George Orwell had written *Nineteen Eighty-Four*. It was a walk at times I thought would never end, or that would end with me being mistaken for a wild stag and shot by one of the many hunters roving the hillsides. But I can recall the moment I rounded a bend and saw the white stone house appear, just like the white whale had appeared to Captain Ahab, and the way my heart had quickened and my confidence returned. This feeling was the same. Yes, it's just the site of an old factory, and one no longer even really there, but this is where my family's modest affluence was earned and where Australia's egalitarian dream came closest to fulfilment before the economic reformers threw cold water in our faces. Such places are just as important as any disused mine or former bank building.

Inside the new warehouse, up in Barry's office, you get a top-tier view of what's replaced the assembly line. It's actually quite spectacular, and it's almost hard to believe that the old assembly line building was half as big again as this. Around 150 people now work on the floor, and another 100 or thereabouts in administration – a fraction of the old payroll list. Barry, who is an expert in warehousing – which I find to be a far more sophisticated industry than I had imagined – quickly estimates the floor sizes of the new buildings springing up on the old GMH site, and calculates that the entire site will be lucky to ever reach 400 jobs, in addition to those at HSPO – a net loss of just under 4000 unionised, well-paid and mostly skilled and semi-skilled working-class jobs to the Dandenong and Doveton area from this site alone. You don't have to be a statistician to draw some important conclusions from that.

Barry generously takes me down onto the floor. As we wander around the vast, quiet space, it is obvious this is still a good place to work – safe, clean, calm, polite and unhurried. It seems efficient in the proper sense of getting things done, rather than in the modern managerialist sense of making people redundant. We see where the trucks bring in containers and pallets of spare parts each morning, where the forklifts take them to the endless rows of scientifically arranged shelves (which remind me of the last scene in *Raiders of the Lost Ark*), and where the ordered parts are sent to dealers and repair centres in the afternoon.

The managers seem a decent lot; it's more like an office than a factory. And yet ... something's missing. What is it? The movement, the noise, the urgency and pace; the energy-sapping overtime that you need an extra-long sleep on Saturday to recover from but which can double your weekly pay packet; even the conflict, the union meetings and the strikes – all are gone. What's missing is the sense of work and life as being more than a tranquil, powerless, well-ordered, well-behaved and highly productive shuffle to the grave.

Work and life should be more than this. They should involve an assertion of rights, a sense of power, a feeling of being part of something bigger – a movement to change things for the better. In an era that has lost religion, life itself should have this sort of religious dimension. It's as if the new economy has done a deal with its workforce: a little more pay in return for your pride, purpose, freedom and the jobs of your friends. It's like one of those H. G. Wells utopias, in which everyone appears happy but bored, and all the hard work is being done by a race of helots hidden somewhere deep underground; in our case, I guess that means in China.

I imagine all sorts of people will know what I mean – journalists missing the once mad activity of the newspaper office, with its drinking and deadlines and passions; aircrew watching their aircraft being piloted by computers; Japanese waiters watching food being served up by a sushi train. That will, of course, sound crazy and romantic and probably plain stupid to the managerialists, and it sometimes does even to me, but I can't help thinking that there's more to life than bland, well-ordered, managed efficiency – the type of life the great captains of industry want to see everyone under them living but couldn't possibly live themselves. Anyone who knows the pampered rich understands that, even more than all their money, it's the conflicts and triumphs of the business world that give them satisfaction and meaning. Their lives are full of passion and struggle; their employees are expected to shut up and obey. That's what defeat looks like.

Barry has one more thing to show me. As we walk towards it, I remark on the cleanliness of the floor, which, as the cliché goes, looks like you could eat off it and not get sick. I hadn't expected that, having worked in many factories myself years ago and seen filthy drains, rats and deadly spiders everywhere. He says it's not the original floor. You see, when the old assembly line building was demolished, it was decided not to jackhammer up the rough, uneven old base but instead to cover it with sand and top it with three feet of smooth, new, sealed concrete. (*Sous les pavés, la plage! Under the paving stones, the beach!*) It's an archaeologist's dream, like a brontosaur falling into a tar pit, and I tell him that thousands of years from now, if humankind is still around, and if all the written records of our time have rotted away and the digital archives have become corrupted or unreadable, someone may rip up this smooth floor and wonder what had changed, what sort of civilisation that concrete from 1999 had covered over.

We reach what Barry wants to show me: a giant mural of the plant from the late 1960s or early '70s, which he had personally saved from destruction when the old plant was being closed down. He's proud of it, and so he should be. There, smiling down on the workers from the far wall of the massive space, is their past. An amateur and not completely successful painting, it is at once industrial and verdant: a huge saw-tooth-roofed factory, with smoke coming from its boiler house chimney, standing in the middle of a vast semi-rural landscape that the city and its economy had yet to completely swallow up. Here was life in the industrial age, an age when not-so-dark and not-so-satanic mills sustained a life much different from the one we live today.

For some reason, the painting reminds me of those pastoral works by Poussin and others, where the happy and innocent peasants frolic among the revegetating ruins of a once great civilisation. Instead of being wantonly smashed to pieces by a ball on a chain, ground up with the factory's bricks and dumped somewhere as contaminated landfill, the picture hints at a life we no longer have – one many might argue was, in important ways, far better.

CHAPTER 2
THE SUBURB THAT WAS MURDERED

We look before and after,
And pine for what is not ...
—PERCY BYSSHE SHELLEY

A t the centre of any great place to work is a top-rate subsidised cafeteria. Anyone who has ever worked in a large organisation, with the possible exception of the federal parliament, can tell you this. Just ask a journalist in a great newspaper, a student in a great college, a machine operator in a great factory. The cafeteria is the place you look forward to, a place to escape the job for an all too brief moment, talk with friends, have a cup of tea and of course eat. Boyfriends and girlfriends eye each other across the tables, dates are arranged, hens' and bucks' nights are organised, wedding invitations are handed out, and photographs of babies and grandchildren are swapped.

The H. J. Heinz factory in Dandenong, just next door to the GMH plant, had a truly great cafeteria, and for twenty years beginning in 1972 my mother operated the cash register there, which put her at the heart of a self-contained little world. As you entered the factory, waving at the security guards as you passed through the gate, the cafeteria stood to the left. You couldn't miss it; it was another of those 1950s modernist designs that would have looked as appealing to the assembly line workers back then as the palatial entry halls of office towers do to accountants and merchant bankers today. (Today the professionals work amid beauty, while workers toil in cheap, functional, concrete prefab boxes; it wasn't always so one-sided.)

I have in front of me the official record from the factory's opening ceremony, held on 7 November 1955 and attended by Prime Minister Robert Menzies. A whole page is given over to what are called STAFF AMENITIES.

> Modern and pleasant staff amenities are provided, with an entire building devoted to this purpose. In this building are lockers, toilet rooms, showers, etc., with each employee provided with an individual locker; a Cafeteria with a seating capacity for 500 people and where a wide variety of food is served, providing a pleasant and restful room for all employees to enjoy lunch and tea-time breaks. A well-equipped First-Aid section is included in this building and a qualified nursing staff is maintained whenever the factory is in operation. With this new Factory providing every modern facility, we look

forward to a long and prosperous association with the communities of Berwick and Dandenong.

The Heinz cafeteria: paradise to parking lot . . .

What strikes you from this passage – apart from the fact it is written in clear prose, not the public-relations jargon of today – is the lengths to which companies like Heinz felt they had to go in order to impress unskilled factory hands. We must remember that factories like these were built in an era when capitalists knew they had to be nice to working-class people if they wanted them to work for them, and when they still felt a moral obligation of sorts to make their employees feel happy; at the very least, they calculated that happiness would make their employees more industrious. Note that the cafeteria had to be 'pleasant', and that breaks were to be 'enjoyed'. Can you imagine a workplace for the working class being designed with such sentiments in mind now? Another era indeed.

In the cafeteria, tea and coffee were free, and three meals were served a day, including a cooked breakfast if you were the sort who could get to work early enough. You could get a three-course meal at the lunch and evening sittings, including soup, full roast dinner with choice of meat, potatoes, fresh vegetables and salads, plus dessert. Many people regularly had their main meal at work because they liked it so much. I remember the cafeteria well because I once regularly ate there too.

For working-class university students like me back in the early to mid-1980s, the end of semester meant one thing: shift work. Education had opened our eyes to wider possibilities, and lying on the beach in Queensland with my new friends would obviously have been far preferable, but the money was fabulous – or at least it seemed so at the time – and turning it down was inconceivable. (This was, of course, in the days before universities got so expensive that even middle-class students had to work in low-paid service industry jobs all year round.) In retrospect, I feel fortunate, because across many sites, sometimes for up to six months at a time, I got to know factory life.

One day during the summer holidays leading up to my third year of university, my mother happened to tell the head of the factory laboratory while he was paying for his lunch that her student son was looking for work; did he have anything suitable? It just so happened that he did, and soon afterwards I found myself part of the tomato season casual intake. The word *laboratory* probably leads you to think I was filling test tubes in an antiseptic room alongside scientists. Wrong; I was a sort of go-between for the lab and the production floor.

My task was to operate a huge industrial kettle the size of a delivery van. Perhaps seven or eight times a day I would climb up a metal staircase, pour a bucket of a selected variety of tomatoes into the kettle (for some reason I remember UC-82s, which were oblong and harder than ordinary tomatoes), add given amounts of water, reduce them down to a set volume of pulp – a process which took around half an hour – and run a sample from it through the factory to the lab, where it would be analysed for sugar levels, viscosity and other qualities that would help make better tomato sauce and baked beans.

As factory jobs went, it had its benefits. On my way to the lab with my tomato samples I could stop and talk to my sister Dawn, who worked with her friends on the packing line watching cans full of cooked food move along a clanking conveyor belt. (My other sister, Pamela, worked at the Cadbury factory.) I could wave to my mother's partner, Fred (my parents had separated in the mid-1970s), who was a forklift driver. Or I could talk to one of the young female lab assistants my mother seemed to approve of more than my then girlfriend. Occasionally I would get squirted with water by one of the factory cleaners, who later served as a minister in the Rudd government.

While the tomato pulp was boiling down, there was little to do apart from tidying up and filling in a few forms, which enabled me to catch up on my university homework, so in fifteen- to twenty-minute blocks I would be standing up high on my machinery in my white overalls, working boots and earplugs (it was a loud factory, which I thought explained why my sisters always seemed to yell at each other, even when they were being friendly) and reading political philosophers like Karl Marx. I still have one of those books – an edited edition of *The Grundrisse* (in essence, the outline of *Das Kapital*) – which is stained with splatters of tomato sauce. (Flicking through it again now, I can see that this is where Marx outlined his own theory about the creative destruction inherent in capitalism, which Schumpeter developed further.)

Even at the time I thought it both an absurd and ironic image: the young proletarian intellectual reading Marx as he operated the very capital that was stealing his surplus value. But when you think about it, there's probably no better place to read socialist philosophy than on the factory floor, and no place more likely to make you realise that while working-class people could be bolshie at times, they were not natural revolutionaries. (Marx, of course, turned out to be partly wrong: my factory workmates were staunch Labor voters, and perhaps this groundedness explains why a lefty like me stayed in the moderate Left of the Labor Party, while the upper-class Marxists I knew at university slummed it for a while in Trotskyist sects before selling out and entering business.)

Back in the cafeteria, my mother was taking on capitalism much more effectively, not with revolutionary philosophy but with kindness. Her blind eye was routinely turned to the most important of rules. She always gave me too much change from my lunch, which everyone else knew full well and laughed at. Anyone who was short of cash to pay for their meals – usually younger workers who would blow their pay well before the end of the week – was fed nonetheless with mountainous portions and given an honour system; Mum simply recorded their debts in her little black book and entered the transaction on pay day. No one ever failed to pay. The manager knew of this ruse but officially pretended not to.

This sort of spirit was the oil that kept the factory running: people who had to suddenly leave work for an hour for important family or medical reasons were covered by their friends; those coming in late were occasionally clocked on and off by others on their shifts. If Fred had to start early, for instance, the managers looked the other way while he ducked home in the car to pick up Mum, who couldn't drive, so she could be there when the breakfast shift ended. Family members and friends were given jobs. (Do they call it nepotism at the big law firms and broking houses when the partners give their children a placement, then a job and then a partnership in the business?) Looking at the old factory newsletters today, a few things catch my eye.

> BIRTHS To Dawn Sutherland (filling floor) and
> Andrew a daughter Tenisha. Grand-daughter to
> Audrey Glover (canteen cashier).

That's the announcement of the birth of my sister Dawn's
first baby, my first niece, in 1989.

> RETIREES Max Moore (fitter and turner Factory
> Engineering). Max gave more than 24 years' service to
> the company and almost as many as a shop steward
> representing his fellow employees. A tough negotiator,
> Max was principled and caring. He has purchased a
> new car and intends to spend some time travelling the
> country during his retirement.

That was the union rep – a part of the team, for all his
faults. It's a good bet his new car had snaked past Dad on
the assembly line in the GMH plant a few hundred yards
away. He could drive it across Australia knowing it gave
employment to his neighbours and friends.

> THE NIGHT OWLS Engineering back shift consists
> of a team of 12 people under the supervision of Doug
> Tarbeck, with Roger Venn as Leading Hand. Including
> Roger there are four fitters, three trade assistants, an
> electrician and a greaser plus three services personnel,
> a boiler attendant, trimmer and a pump house
> attendant. It may be the nature of the job, or the

people themselves, but working while others have gone to bed seems to encourage a certain independence of thought and self-reliance. Perhaps they become used to decision-making and sorting things out for themselves.

What follows are details of how the twelve had streamlined the night shift production processes, saving the company serious money. Here, the skills of working people and their contribution to efficiency and profit was well recognised by the management team. They didn't have degrees but it seemed they knew what they were doing and did it well.

There are also stories about the success of the three Heinz netball teams, the Heinz women's indoor cricket team, the Heinz running team and the twenty separate Heinz ten-pin bowling teams, whose season culminated in a grand final and an awards night at which everyone got a trophy; these factory workers didn't bowl alone. A long story covers the fun had at the end-of-tomato-season 'Academy Awards Night' for departing casual workers, organised by permanently employed volunteers. Even the casuals were treated like human beings by having their service acknowledged; often, if the managers could keep them on, they did.

Our little community's strengths extended beyond the factory gate. At bingo nights at the Dandenong Workers' Club, where many of the factory workers were members, someone in hard financial times might suddenly find that they had won the jackpot. When economists and accountants make up numbers to prove their absurd theories or mislead the taxman, society is the loser; at Heinz the faked figures were on the side of the angels.

That's how life was for the 1200 souls (up to 1600 at the peak of the tomato season) in the republic of Heinz back then. The economic reformers today would scoff and label their community-minded antics as inefficiency, luxury and 'entitlement', and some of the more ideological analysts at right-wing think-tanks like the Centre for Independent Studies or the Institute of Public Affairs might even call it 'theft', but it's hard to see how such trifling indulgences could sink so large a battleship as Heinz. Indeed, the original calculation was that the sort of friendly work environment Heinz created and tolerated for so long would build a strong, loyal and hardworking workforce, and it's my bet that was right. But when the creative destroyers seized economic power in Canberra and began looking for award trade-offs, all that human decency, all that loyalty – all those things they couldn't measure and therefore regarded as worthless – had to go. What gets measured gets improved, as they say; everything else gets vaporised.

In 1992 the Heinz workforce was halved, and a few years later halved again. Dawn had already left to become a full-time mother, although she returned for seasonal work. Mum took a package at about this time. Fred took his in

1997, after thirty-five years of service. And then in 2000 the factory closed its gates for good. Seven weeks' pay and four weeks' for every year, up to a total of fifteen. So a maximum of sixty-seven weeks' pay – not bad for those who found other work straightaway, but for many it was the last full-time, permanent job they ever had. As Shakespeare might have put it: *This happy breed of men and women, this little world, this precious stone set in the silver sea ... this blessed plot, this factory, this company, this Doveton. All now gone.*

Like the Holden plant, you can still find the Heinz factory: you turn down a laneway off 'Progress Way' in Dandenong. The guardhouse is gone but you can still make out where it used to stand. The footpath we all once took into the factory proper is still there. It used to take you to the changing rooms and the clock-on point, where you would press your card into the slot with a *kerthump*, before filing it on the wall. Now it's just empty tarmac; in fact, I realise soon after stepping out of the car that I am standing pretty much on top of the cafeteria. It's a parking lot. Joni Mitchell wrote a song about this sort of thing.

The space has changed so much since I worked here thirty years before that I find it hard to visualise where everything once was. Panda has come with me and is just as perplexed as me. At a large factory building his politician's charm gets him talking to a young guy, who tells us he rents the space as a warehouse for his small business, which distributes the Yellow Pages to the surrounding suburbs. He seems genuinely sympathetic to our nostalgic quest to find out what had happened to the place, so he offers me a fluoro vest and tells me to feel free to walk around and take photographs; 'just pop the vest back when you finish.'

As at Holden, I can see one or two people rattling around in the cavernous space. At the far end, which is leased by another company, trucks can be seen coming and going, but again there are only a handful of employees to be seen where once hundreds would have swarmed. We find that the old R&D building – where new food products and their marketing strategies were once devised – is now a logistics training space for Toll. Below the roof line you can still make out the words 'Research and Development', although the sign that once hung there is long gone.

R&D – we used to do that . . .

Amid it all, where the Dry Goods building stood and barrels of cucumbers and crates of tomatoes once awaited canning, there is now a Hino trucks distribution and spare parts centre. I walk into the showroom and ask a friendly older man at the counter what he knows about the site. Not much, he says. I ask him how many people he sees walking around the site each day. He can't really say, but he reckons that about forty or so work there for Hino. At least 1200 people once made things here; now well under 100 on-sell things made in places like China.

On my second visit I take Fred. Having driven a forklift around the site for more than thirty-five years, he calmly walked around it with me, pointing: 'Sterilising, labelling and packing were there ... The two-storey kitchen was next to that ... The boiler house beyond that, at the end of the site.' Some of the original buildings remain. The Yellow Pages warehouse had been the Finished Goods Store. 'And over there,' he says, 'is where *you* worked.' It was the Preparation Shed.

Ignoring the 'Do Not Enter' signs, I walk in. (In warehousing, it seems, the best camouflage colours are fluorescent yellow and orange.) Yes, he's right. In fact, I can see the very spot where my little piece of surplus-value-extracting capital had been fixed to the floor, and where my Marxism had started to evaporate along with the tomato pulp. The familiar saw-toothed roof, with its thousands of square feet of glass, is intact, the dirty machinery is gone and the floor stretches out pristine, functionless

and worker-free except for one or two men chatting next
to an exceedingly clean-looking truck.

Where my machine stood . . .

My bearings restored, I could now see it all again: sauces,
beans, tomatoes and soups plopping into the sterilised
cans; Dawn and her friends labelling and packing them
after the lids were closed; Fred lifting them with his forklift onto trucks and off to the supermarket; Mum further
beyond in the Cafeteria keeping the crew happy and con-
tented; all well with our little world.

Some of the Heinz buildings remain, but what became
of the people? I know about Mum, Fred and Dawn, of
course, but what of the others? I am given a great chance
to find out because I've been invited to the five-yearly reunion of the factory's former employees. Despite the fact
that the place closed fifteen years ago, the old social club
committee still has 800 people on its books, nearly 400 of

whom have managed to make it. The venue – the Berwick Bowls Club – looks eerily familiar; I realise I've been here before, having watched Kim Beazley deliver a speech I'd helped write on the evening of 9/11; he was still on his feet when the first tower came down and snuffed out any hope he'd had of winning the forthcoming election. That's another story, of course, but had those planes missed those towers, things here might not have turned out so badly. Perhaps Kim would have made it more bearable.

I move around the room, chatting to people and taking notes. I meet people who worked at Heinz for twenty-eight years, thirty-five years and forty years. I meet the man who closed the gates on the day the plant closed; another who had been made redundant and was then re-hired the next year to demolish the buildings, which took three years. He did well out of it, having received a hefty redundancy payout and plenty of super, followed by a job, but he tells me he'd have preferred to have kept his original job. I talk to people from Baby Foods, people from Marketing, people from Payroll who tell me of the gradual winding-down of the place; managers who claim the union's unreal demands were to blame; other managers who tell me the factory needed too much capital injected into it to remain viable, there being asbestos in the roof and the boiler room that had to be removed; and other managers who come clean on the fact that there were un-unionised workers in New Zealand on half the pay and half the holidays and half the conditions (and who, I guess, were probably prepared to eat stale sandwiches in some cold and crummy shed they called a canteen), which made the decision to close a no-brainer. One former tradesman tells me he helped dismantle and ship the 'hydrons' – the giant hydroscopic sterilising units for tin cans – off to New Zealand, where our Heinz products are now largely made. It's the old story: there was more money to be made where labour was cheaper, and it was all the unions' fault. Isn't it always?

I put this to Dawn's friends, the packing girls Cheryl, Anne, Lorene and Louise, whose faces I vaguely remember and who have a different take on what happened. Sure, they had occasionally gone on strike, sometimes over big pay disputes and other times over matters that to the managers seemed trivial – but then the managers weren't earning unskilled wages, and didn't have to work when it was hot in summer, cold in winter and noisy all the time. I quickly realise, though, that the concept of industrial relations – which came naturally to me, having read Marx's early draft of *Das Kapital* up there on my machine – is not what Dawn's friends first think of when they talk of their work at Heinz. In their memories, Heinz wasn't a series of strikes or class struggles, but more like a family. That sounds suspiciously like just the sort of sentimentality you might hear at a reunion after a couple of drinks, but when I pursue the idea I can tell that it is genuinely felt; even the managers say something similar. Being at Heinz, with its steady long-term workforce, its friendly cafeteria that was rather like a lounge room, its social and sporting clubs, its Christmas parties, its friendships and marriages (and divorces) and babies and grandchildren, its share of conflict and tragedies but also of common effort and achievements, its rhythms of soups and spaghetti in winter, tomatoes and overtime in summer, its sheer predictability and employment certainty, its air of being there not just for the boss and the managers and the shareholders but for everyone, was just like being in an extended family.

Dawn's friend Cheryl is the most voluble, although the others are nodding and butting in with comments, and she says she looks back on the closure of the factory with genuine sorrow. So I ask the obvious question: for her, was working life better back then? She stares at me with utter incredulity and says, 'Oh, *yeah!*'

Then it comes out, like a message in a bottle that has just washed ashore and been uncorked. Fifteen years later, instead of working in manufacturing, she's working as a storeman for a labour-hire firm in a warehouse, earning just $17 per hour ($16.86 to be precise, or $640.90 a week; the employers' lobby wanted it to be just $630.70), with no union, no overtime, no real job security and not even a canteen; some fellow employees even have to buy their own safety boots, and no one gets the sort of Christmas bonus they used to get at Heinz. It's no surprise she's not enjoying it much at all. Worst of all, she says, is that as she is now living on her own, without a husband's job to help support her, she can only just get by. Whenever she needs to get ahead, she has to take on a second job – not at double time, not even at time and a half, but at single time (yes, $16.86 per hour). The better life promised to us by all the managerialist politicians and their favourite economists and their boosters in the press clearly hasn't been delivered to everyone.

A few days later I read a front-page story in the *Age* which reports that, after two decades of uninterrupted economic growth, there are now 1.5 million Australians living in poverty. Apparently, we haven't reformed enough yet. Cheryl's story is a narrative more informative and eloquent than statistical abstractions like Gini coefficients could ever hope to be. Her share of GDP has clearly been redistributed elsewhere, perhaps paying the school fees of an accountant living in some leafy suburb she will never afford, and her feeling of inferiority has become someone else's feeling of superiority.

In the last scene of Rob Reiner's terrific coming-of-age film *Stand By Me*, the central character, Gordie Lachance (played by Richard Dreyfus), who has escaped his home town and its constrictions to become a writer, is lamenting the loss of his childhood friend Chris (River Phoenix), who has just been killed in a senseless knife attack in a fast-food restaurant. The death pricks at his memory and inspires him to write the story that becomes the narrative of the film, a story about his old town, told in flashback. Thinking about how to end the story, Gordie turns to his word processor and writes: 'I never had any friends later on like the ones I had when I was twelve. Jesus, does anyone?'

The movie became an instant classic because it appeals to a very human yearning most of us share: to know what has happened to the friends from our childhood. It's the sort of impulse that makes us go to school reunions, often against our better judgment, only to leave early and disappointed. I'm now over fifty, and it's one of the great satisfactions of my life that I've managed to keep in close contact with virtually all of the friends I had when I was twelve.

It's a truism that every cohort passing through a school or college considers itself unique, somehow better than the ones that came before and after. We've all felt this, only to realise later that it was an error induced by perspective. But something tells me that my school friends were indeed extraordinary. Let me tell you about them briefly, because they're central to my story about what's happened to Doveton. Their names and nicknames are the sort you'd expect of boys of that generation: Panda and Jim I've already mentioned, but there was also 'Chook', 'Hen', 'Molesy' (there was an animal theme to our nicknames), Nick, Grant, Dave, Chris, John (who was 'Pommy', for obvious reasons), Henry and George.

For the sons of mostly factory workers they've all done incredibly well, becoming, in the order mentioned above, a state Labor MP and minister, a draughtsman and factory manager, an IT engineer and now small-business owner, a banker, another banker, an insurance executive, another IT engineer, an owner of a labour-hire company, an investor, a park ranger, an international development consultant and an accountant. Their wives, many Doveton girls, have done just as well. Some return to Doveton regularly to look after their ageing parents, but all have more or less left and moved to newer or fancier suburbs, even living overseas for a time in low-tax jurisdictions, and they've educated their children at supposedly better and definitely more expensive schools than our old high school. While I went the furthest academically, most would, I guess, be better off financially than me (and if not, the reason is divorce).

As Panda never forgets to remind us, the Labor Party made much of our success possible. Our old high school – Doveton High, long since flattened to make way for a housing estate – was given special 'disadvantaged schools' funding by Gough Whitlam and by Kim Beazley's father, Kim Beazley senior, and ours was the first cohort of students to benefit fully. Ours was the first in a number of years to be offered the Higher School Certificate – before then, the smarter kids transferred to other schools close by – and after us, the sixth form lasted for only a couple more years, with smaller enrolments and a narrower subject range before it ran out of puff. And when we got to TAFE and university they were free.

Education has taken us far, but the true context that made our upward mobility possible was a local economy that gave every family one or more jobs. Moderate affluence, not economic deregulation, is the magic ingredient that gave us our start, and it can do it for others. In the absence of that moderate affluence in a deregulated world, downward mobility is the result. Doveton used to create success stories like that. The question is: can it do so again?

I'm generally against statistics – you will note their comparative absence in this book – not because of what they tell us, which can sometimes be useful, but because they make it too easy to ignore what is going on in front of our very eyes. It's too tempting, isn't it, to sit in front of a screen in a warm office, look at lines of averages on graphs edging upwards and believe that, for everyone, life is getting better. The big-picture studies so beloved of the managerialists, like those by the National Centre for Social and Economic Modelling (NATSEM), suggest that over the last decade and a half, every section of the population has got wealthier, even if some have got far wealthier than others.

According to NATSEM, the lowest 20 per cent of income earners have seen their standard of living increase by 27.1 per cent since 1985, and even welfare recipients are 11.9 per cent better off (although those who get their income largely from capital saw a rise of 64.8 per cent).

It's abstractions and nationwide averages like this that make us complacent about what's really happening in the places we don't really want to know about. So what do the non-averaged statistics, the ones about places like Doveton, tell us?

Doveton was created by the Victorian Housing Commission in 1955 with the specific goal of providing housing for employees of the Big Three factories of GMH, International Harvester and H. J. Heinz. By its completion in 1966, around 2500 homes had been built. There were certainly plenty of jobs for the families living in them. In 1970 those three factories alone employed the following numbers of people in permanent, full-time jobs: GHM 4500, Heinz 1200, and International Harvester 1750 – a total of 7450. By 1995, this had been reduced to GHM 300, Heinz 350, International Harvester (now the truck manufacturer IVECO) 600, for a total of 1250. In 2015 the totals are GMH (now HSPO) 250, Heinz 0, IVECO 290 – a total of 540. That's a net loss of 6910 permanent, full-time jobs.

	1970	1995	2015
GMH	4500	300	250
International Harvester	1750	600	290
H. J. Heinz	1200	350	0
TOTAL	7450	1250	540

Jobs at the Big Three, 1970–2015

To put it another way, in 1970 there were three jobs in these factories for every Doveton family; by 1995 there was one job for every two families; today there is just one job for every five families. Remember, this is for a community that was created with the specific purpose of housing employees for these three factories. If you take those jobs away but keep the houses there, and if you continue to fill them with the sorts of people who need low-skilled factory jobs, an interesting social experiment begins.

The net result? Consider this: in 1966 the unemployment rate in Doveton was less than 1 per cent (below the national average of just under 2 per cent), by 1991, at the height of the 'recession we had to have', it was 19 per cent (the national average then being around 10 per cent), and in 2015, after no fewer that twenty-three years of uninterrupted economic growth, it stands at 21.1 per cent (the national average being 6.1 per cent). Twenty years after the factories began closing down, the unemployment rate in Doveton is actually higher than during one of the most psychologically destructive recessions since the Great Depression.

During those dark recession years when the economic reform revolution reached its terrible apogee, my father, my mother, my youngest sister and her husband were all made redundant, meaning that four out of eight working adults in my family, all of whom were still living in suburbs adjoining Doveton, lost their jobs. (My brother-in-law, who back then was a unionised auto worker, has only once voted Labor since.) And this does not take into account the fact that the definition of 'unemployment' has changed, making the comparison even worse. In recent years, other jobs have been created in the warehousing and small-scale manufacturing hinterland to the suburb's south, but clearly these jobs have not gone to the people of my old suburb. For places like Doveton, the recovery has been a largely jobless one. That is the problem.

The effect of this on the material quality of life of Doveton's residents has been dramatic. In 1966, 10 per cent were in the lowest income category, by 1991 that had risen to 37 per cent, and in the 2011 Census 34.9 per cent of residents were still classed as 'low-income households' – which means they earned less than $600 per week, or roughly the minimum wage of one working parent. According to the Australian Bureau of Statistics' standard measure of advantage and disadvantage – Socio-Economic Indexes for Areas, or SEIFA – Doveton is now the fourth-most disadvantaged suburb in Victoria.

Perhaps the saddest thing to contemplate is that there are many Dovetons – many once affluent public housing suburbs that were built to support thriving industries, but that have been left behind by the revolution. Doveton itself is probably not even the poorest of them. In Dandenong, immediately next door to Doveton, unemployment is 21.7 per cent. Norlane, a Victorian Housing Commission estate built around the Ford factory in Geelong, has an unemployment rate of 20.7 per cent. Broadmeadows, in Melbourne's

north, another Victorian Housing Commission site, which
is highly dependent on the Ford factory in nearby Camp-
bellfield, has an unemployment rate of 25.7 per cent. Elizabeth, in Adelaide's north, is a South Australian Housing
Trust site, developed in large part for workers in the nearby
Holden factory, and it now has a frightening unemployment rate of 32.6 per cent. Remember, all these car factories
will be gone before the end of 2017, when all Australian car
manufacturing will cease, and their unemployment rates,
which are already as high as or higher than Doveton's, will
be far higher still. These places are potentially heading towards a social catastrophe.

What we have done in places like Doveton is create a
new economic class. It's true that, for many working-class
people, the changes of the past thirty years have been
liberating. We've coined a name for these people – 'aspirationals' – and their success is something to celebrate.
Much has been written about this aspirational class,
which has many fair-weather champions, so I won't detail
its considerable success here, except to say that there are
suburbs full of people like this not far from Doveton, and
obviously many individual examples in Doveton itself.
But while we lavish attention on the aspirationals' success,
we've turned our backs on their former workmates and
neighbours who didn't succeed when the economy was
pulled out from under them. We didn't do enough to help
them succeed, but we should have.

So who are they? I don't like the term 'underclass', with

its condescending connotations of depravity and crime, and its assumption that the victims are themselves to blame for their misfortune. This is not a law-and-order issue but an economic and social issue. 'Housos' is another insulting and degrading epithet – and anyway, this isn't about housing, it's about people. Above all, this is an employment issue. So let's call this class what it really is: the 'non-working class', or perhaps more accurately the 'once-working class'. Our economic revolution has created it, and we collectively bear a moral responsibility to remove the 'non' and the 'once' from its names.

The economic reformers led us to believe – in fact, *promised* would probably not be too strong a word – that greater productivity, by leading to higher economic growth, would make the existence of this sort of class unlikely: that all boats would float as the tide rose and everyone could aspire to something better. Even they couldn't have dreamed that their high tide would last for twenty-three years. But here it is: Australia rich, Doveton and other places like it poor.

A wise person might consider the possibility that the two results might be linked, and that the *way* we have pursued growth has prevented many people in places like Doveton from sharing in the rewards. In the past, people in these places were shielded from the full winds of the market to help us create a fairer and better society, but now the shield has been ripped away and such places have been exposed to a hurricane. This is more than just a quantitative change in our economy – it is a new economy without a heart or conscience. We used to create wealth by including places like Doveton; now we create wealth by excluding them. And in doing so, could it be that we've changed our economy in some fundamental way, without fully realising the import of what we are doing, removing not just the goal of equality from our calculations but re-moving moral considerations more generally? And could it be that in doing so, we've changed ourselves as a people? This is what the aggregated national statistics don't tell us.

Doveton is the suburb that was murdered. And it is not alone. Its continuing existence is an embarrassment to the economic reformers because it proves that their theo-ries were either wrong or heartless. When the suburb's factories shut, Doveton suffered a mini depression that, like a runaway steamroller, smashed everything in its path. That steamroller is still on the loose across the land. Other places got the creation, but Doveton and places like it got the destruction. Twenty years on, little has changed, as I was to see.

CHAPTER 3

GROUND ZERO

What powerful but unrecorded race
Once dwelt in that annihilated place?
— HORACE SMITH

The word *trespass* has far more ethical meaning than it deserves. Simply by erecting a sign saying 'Do Not Enter', the state or the corporation puts into your mind the idea of transgression. Go through that broken gate, squeeze your way through that gap in the builder's fence, stride confidently past a momentarily empty security office and you become a sort of moral outlaw. But a 'Do Not Enter' sign might also alert you to something someone else doesn't want you to know about.

The Endeavour Hills Secondary College was once called Doveton North Technical School. It opened in 1969 to train boys to do the jobs of their fathers by preparing them for apprenticeships – or at least for the discipline of the time clock – at the Big Three. My friend Dave, with whom I used to open the batting, went here. Today, it's the sort of place the economic reformers don't want you to see. Here is the epicentre of creative destruction, the Ground Zero of Professor Schumpeter's dark vision.

The first thing you notice as you enter the school today – which you do by bending double to pass though a hole smashed in one of its doors – is the unnerving crunch of broken glass under your feet. In retrospect, it shouldn't come as much of a surprise, since the desolate playground is littered with unwanted mattresses, paint tins and other hard-to-dispose-of rubbish. Still, nothing can prepare you for what's to come, especially when you think to yourself that this is Australia, not some American city like Detroit where people don't really count.

In the early 1980s, when Ronald Reagan was deploying cruise missiles on the borders of the Soviet Union, a new genre of movie appeared, set in the nuclear Armageddon. You might remember some examples: *Threads*, *The Day After*, *When the Wind Blows*. The most disturbing thing about these movies wasn't the physical destruction they showed but their belief that a post-nuclear society would descend into some sort of chaotic lunacy, a kingdom of the insane brought under control by a modern version of feudalism, ruled by street gangs.

Perhaps because I was fascinated by these films (a fascination which started when a teacher at Doveton High showed us Peter Watkins' then shocking mock documentary, *The War Game*), the first word that comes to my mind as I enter the school building and stare down the main corridor is *apocalypse*. Down all four corridors of the main block – which consists of three parallel chambers about fifty metres long, connected mid-section by a shorter fourth one – every wall has been defaced by the warnings of street gangs, and literally every panel of glass smashed. Between elaborately painted tags, there are the usual obscenities and crude symbols of people being hung by the neck. In almost every classroom the walls have been roughly removed, as if some army of psychopathic home renovators had set to them with long-handled hammers. Here and there floorboards have been ripped up, the better to get to the copper wires and the recently installed fibre-optic cabling. In one of the central courtyards, a large, twisted pile of coloured tubing of various diameters is evidence of the building's nocturnal disembowelling; perhaps there's money in it.

Particular attention has been paid to the entrance hall, which looks like a high-street bank frontage that has been ram-raided by a truck. Next to it is a large yellow arrow, possibly put there to manage the traffic when the place was still alive with the shouts and movement of teenagers. Over the arrow, some illegal visitor – who knows, perhaps a grammatically challenged former student, now unemployed – has spray-painted the words 'IF U WANT 2 DIE, THIS WAY, FUCKERS!' (I've added the commas to make the meaning clear.) It's not as pleasant as the slogans about flagstones and beaches the Parisian students wrote on the walls of the Sorbonne in 1968 but it's rather more direct. In one classroom, the day's lesson – on how to make a rebate joint, a skill that could help some youngster get a job in the building trade – is still in chalk on the blackboard.

The entrance hall – after the apocalypse . . .

A classroom – newly renovated . . .

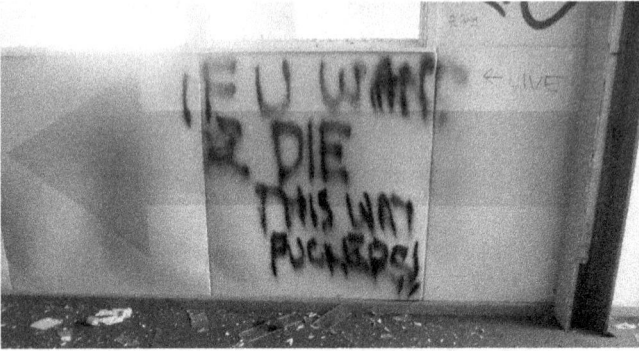

A slogan for Professor Schumpeter . . .

Lessons for us all . . .

Perhaps the strangest thing about the insides of the now destroyed school is the feeling of newness. Between the holes and the graffiti and under the broken glass and cables, everything is in nearly mint condition. There appears to have been a very recent and major fit-out, leaving behind new classroom partitions, pristine whiteboards, rows of

Disembowelment...

shattered toilets that are still sparkling white, walls yet to be turned grubby by the rubbing of teenage shoulders, and carpet not yet muddied by dirty shoes. It's as if the whole place was scrubbed clean for its execution, like a sacrificial infant at the temple of a Mayan sun god.

The insides of this dying building are so breathtaking that they induce in me a variety of blood-pumping excitement; after all, it's not impossible, and perhaps even not unlikely, that some ice-crazed adolescent might appear around a corner at any moment with a knife. It's only when I crawl outside again that my sense of melancholy returns. There, in front of me, is an old soccer field, the grandstand burnt down and razed by council bulldozers as a safety precaution, the pitch alternately bare and weedy. Behind the main building is the vocational education block, similarly smashed and defaced. They once taught young people skills for the auto trades here; now, having decided to leave car manufacturing jobs to the Germans, French, English, Koreans, Thais and Chinese, we can safely leave public assets like this in ruins. At least the economists will be happy, because the otherwise unused land is now being put to the most efficient use their collective wisdom has been able to devise: as a junkyard.

As I walk away from the school, scale its fence and look back, I notice that it is slowly being overtaken by nature. Weeds sprout from every garden bed, concrete crack and gutter like those reclaiming the Roman forum in the famous etchings by Piranesi. Parts of the roof are disappearing; whether blown off or stolen it's hard to tell. Soon the rain will be getting in, the walls will be getting damp and the place will be unsafe to enter. If you've ever read John Wyndham's classic novel *The Day of the Triffids*, you'll know that its best scene is the one where the protagonist travels back to London years after the apocalypse, only to find it reclaimed by nature, its pavements choked by spreading weeds, turf growing on roofs, tree roots undermining buildings and branches poking through smashed windows. That's Doveton North Tech today, once proud but now an abandoned ruin, slowly disappearing beneath nature's onslaughts.

There is, however, one surface in the complex that remains untouched by the hands of the vandals. It is the sign boasting that the now completely wrecked and abandoned school received money from the stimulus plan that followed the global financial crisis. 'Nation Building – Economic Stimulus Plan,' it reads, in the sort of dubious English that the managerialists who devised the plan love so much, 'supporting jobs and rebuilding our infrastructure for the future.' It seems the school had been given a major renovation and refit just before it was closed.

A nation-building project . . .

Here is the Building the Education Revolution plan at work. Its inspiration, John Maynard Keynes, once said that in a recession the most rational thing to do is pay people to bury sacks full of pound notes in disused mineshafts, and then pay the same people to dig them up again. This could have been the sort of thing he meant. Having read that morning in the *Financial Review* that the market for collateralised debt obligations is once again booming, I muse that perhaps when the next financial crisis comes we can dig up the buried foundations of this school as yet another Keynesian make-work project.

While I'm taking photographs of the sign, a Vietnamese-Australian couple pull up in their car, taking me (again in my fluoro vest and hardhat) for a council employee. When is the council going to sell the site, they ask, because they want to buy the land and build apartments on it. I tell them I have no idea, but that some of my friends went to school here and it's still owned by the Department of Education, and everyone knows they move at a snail's pace. Might be years! They leave disappointed.

The strange fact that the sign remains seems a symbol of something important, although it's not easy to say precisely what. A bureaucratic stuff-up, perhaps? Evidence, maybe, that the bureaucrats who closed the school have a strong sense of irony? Or proof that, when it all comes down to it, no one *really* cares what happens in Doveton, and that the destruction of places like this doesn't even count as a source of political embarrassment? That's my guess. What we do know is that the government public-relations expert who once commanded the sign to be raised couldn't even be bothered to order it taken down.

I take one last look at the sign before driving off to another abandoned school site – this time my old primary school, which is in a similar state of neglect. To my surprise, I find it surrounded by a three-metre-high fence, which must have been erected after I exposed the school's scandalous state in the national press the year before. I later take Panda back to it, and we walk across the remains of the old adventure playground where we first became friends. He tells me that at least people are listening, even if the only effect has been to encourage officials to try to hide the place from view.

As I scale the old school gate to cross the road to have a look at my cousins' old house – which is in a state almost as shocking as that of my own old family home – I look back to the school and think of Shelley and his romantic poet friends who had something to tell us about forgotten civilisations. Around the decay of that colossal wreck, boundless and bare, the lone and level sands of official indifference stretch far away.

If a picture paints a thousand words, then the image of a shuttered shop is an essay in social decline. You can see the shutters by day, up high, wound around their covered rollers like aluminium foil in its cardboard box. But at night they come down with a rattle and a thump, in a noisy indictment of a society that has gone wrong.

There are no shutters above the frontages in the wealthier shopping strips, despite there being a lot more to steal; go to Albert Park, for example, and you won't see them at all. (For this we can thank supply-side economics, which helpfully supplies depressed neighbourhoods with necessary numbers of the young, the unemployed, the drug-addicted and the idle.)

And from memory there were no shutters in our shopping strip when I was a child. It's five minutes' walk from my old street, and about three from my primary school. My mother worked on the cash register in the milk bar; it must have been before 1972, when she started at Heinz. Walking back into the milk bar now evokes the strangest feeling, because while it has changed completely, it has yet remained completely unchanged.

I remember the glass counters full of stock of all descriptions – lollies which we used to buy in five-cent mixed bags, tea, coffee, biscuits, cakes, breakfast cereals, cheese and cold meats. There was a big metal meat slicer, from which my mother would produce slithers of sweet ham or continental sausage into our palms when the shop's owner wasn't looking. A large freezer contained Peters and Streets ice creams, and cheap toys stood on the shelves on the wall behind the counter, which Mum would occasionally buy for us as small treats. It was never a fashionable delicatessen; perhaps closer to a bright and cheery 7-Eleven. But now ...

The best word I can use to describe the old milk bar now is *poor* – in the economic sense. Looking around, it seems not a lick of paint has touched its walls for half a century. My guess is that the only thing in the place that has been replaced is the refrigerator – which was probably made in China. The floor, then brightly coloured concrete, adorned with painted footprints advertising a now defunct childhood confectionary, has been discoloured and worn down in the places of highest traffic, like the stone floors in ancient churches. The almost empty shelves are watched over by a proprietor who, I guess from the kitchen-like smells of the place, might live out the back.

On my first visit back to the shop I get chatting to the cashier. I figure she's most likely the proprietor, as it's hard to see how any shop as poor as this could possibly support a living wage; it has to be family-run. I tell her how my mother once worked here, and how I haven't been into the shop for about thirty years. When I say the shop hasn't changed much, she tells me in return that the neighbourhood has changed enormously over that time. It's no longer safe, she said, and I should be careful walking around, even though it's only mid-morning.

As I walk down the strip and drink my Coke, I see a policeman photographing the smashed window of one of the adjoining stores. A young man with the broken physique one normally associates with severe addiction approaches me for a strange conversation about daytime television; he soon walks off, carrying a six-pack of pre-mixed drinks. The danger seems more comic than scary; I can't imagine feeling afraid in a place like this, where I'd felt so safe as a child, but then I don't live there anymore. And the cause of rational fear is, after all, cumulative negative experience.

The next time I come back, a year later, the shop has changed completely. Not the décor, which is still untouched, but the food shelves, whose contents have been replaced by the cheapest junk from the crummiest factories in the world. The milk bar is now a mixed business, part milk bar, part plastic junk from Bangladesh or China. Outside, a lonely sandwich board stands on the footpath, looking like it has been painted by a child. It reads: '$2 Shop.'

At least there's only one $2 shop here. At the bigger shopping strip on the other side of Doveton I count three of them, plus a charity store run by one of the bigger welfare agencies. I recognised one of the $2 shops as the baby and children's clothing store that my aunt, Anna, had run back in the late 1960s and early '70s. The clothes she sold would almost certainly have been produced here in Australia. A lot of my and my sisters' childhood clothes came from there, made by women working in factories in Melbourne's northern suburbs.

That thought reminded me of a conversation with another aunt, Ena (one of Arthur Calwell's original beautiful blonde Baltic refugees who came here in the late 1940s), who told me how, when she worked as a salesgirl in the Dandenong Coles Variety Store back in the mid-1960s, she used to sell the very garments that her mother had stitched in a clothing factory in Bendigo. Thank God such things as clothes are all now made in Bangladesh, because the law of comparative advantage tells us clearly that there's no need for us to make them here, and it would be a sin to contradict the law of comparative advantage.

At the end of the strip is a real-estate agent's office that used to be a branch of the Commonwealth Bank. In its window there is a listing for one of the shops, a rather well-presented fruit and vegetable store, for sale to bids over $50,000. A whole double-fronted shop, with two car spaces, going for just north of fifty grand? In the inner city, just renovating a café or a restaurant might set you back a million.

The old Doveton Post Office is now owned or leased by some evangelical sect, which, no doubt in addition to undertaking sundry unspecified good works, believes in speaking in tongues, divine healing, a real physical hell and the imminent second coming of Jesus. They also post their BSB and account details on their website in case you want to make an electronic funds transfer to help out with the battle against Satan. Later, I come across a similar church squatting in a vandalised building in a street where an ancient factory once stood and a woman was savagely murdered last year. An economic development officer tells me that evangelical sects have targeted Doveton because of the cheap rents, and that one of the pastors here is infamous for inciting hatred of Muslims.

As I walk around the shopping centre, having bought in one of the $2 shops a $10 soccer ball for my sons (the stitching of which lasts just a few days), I think unkind thoughts about economic reformers. But isn't it refreshing to know that they have so successfully liberated all of us from the pathetically unsophisticated lives, crummy consumer goods and poverty of our past? The unemployment rate here in Doveton is ten times that of the wealthiest suburbs, and fully two or three times that of some other very proletarian-sounding places. And we're thirty years into an era of economic reform that was meant to make us all better off!

Then it strikes me: it's Doveton and other places like it that have paid the price for the gains the rest of country has made. It's only because places like Doveton are smashed up – their old communities dispersed, their factories closed, their unions broken, their skilled craftsmen forced to work two menial jobs to make ends meet, their political leaders left morally bereft and philosophically rudderless, their youngsters unemployed and drinking before midday, their cheery little corner stores turned into $2 shops, their front yards turned into scrapyards and their schools stripped of the metal from their roofs and the cables from their floors – that everyone else feels so prosperous. It's because of all the sacrifices that the people of Doveton have involuntarily made that people in more affluent places get to drive their Audis and BMWs, build their schools new campuses in China, send their boys on cricket tours of England and their daughters on gallery expeditions to Paris, make their children the leaders of tomorrow, convert their income to capital and super, rake in franked dividends from their Commonwealth Bank and Telstra shares, shop in New York, own five investment properties, and get their accountants to arrange it all so the taxman – so willing nowadays to turn a blind eye – doesn't know the half of it. It's only because

Doveton is down that they are up, because Doveton is poor that they are rich, because Doveton has been made to feel inferior that they can feel effortlessly superior. Every coin has a flipside, every gain has a cost; for every winning team there's a losing one, for every Hawthorn and Point Piper and North Adelaide and Peppermint Grove there's a Doveton.

By coming to places like Doveton, you see plainly that wealth isn't just created, it's distributed, and you understand that the way it's created determines the way it's distributed. You see that in order for the economic reformers to unchain the nation, Doveton had to be placed in chains. And it's time Australia and its leaders owned up to the logic of what they've done.

We're constantly told that this sort of thinking isn't the way we should go; that it's 'class warfare' and 'the politics of envy', and that it seeks to drag others down when the goal is to lift everyone up. But that's a cheap and easy line and nothing more, because Doveton and places like it remind us that while the economy has been unchained for thirty years, the reformers' promise of lifting everyone up hasn't been fulfilled, and places like Doveton have actually gone backwards. If there's been an outbreak of envy, it's among the well-off who envy the unemployed for their dole and welfare payments, which they have savagely reduced to help even up the score.

It didn't have to be this way. We could have modernised differently, with a little more thought for what was going to happen to the people at the bottom, the people for whom our now destroyed old society had been built. The Labor Party, at least, should have thought about this. Now it's time to choose another way.

Shuttered shops . . .

Bouncing my ball, I make my way back to my car. I take out my camera and lean on the bonnet, looking over at the shops, hoping to get a shot of the shutters coming down; it's already after five. But of course for the owners of such shops, the long day doesn't end at the traditional closing hour.

Something about it all makes me want to rebel, but my sadness is impotent in the face of a decline so profound and irreversible. I can't reopen the factories and give Cheryl and her workmates back their overtime, or restore my old streets, schools and shopping strips to their former, sunny glory. A writer – even one who is politically well connected like me – can do little except put words in a speech, and those are easily ignored and forgotten, even when spoken by a prime minister. How, I wonder, has it all been allowed to happen without anyone in power saying, 'Enough'?

The answer is simple: there was a revolution. We just called it something else.

CHAPTER 4
THE LOST REVOLUTION

Wild Spirit, which art moving everywhere;
Destroyer and preserver ...
  —PERCY BYSSHE SHELLEY

The smart backpacker chooses his travel reading carefully, preferably a single paperback equivalent in size to *War and Peace*. That's how in 1985 I ended up reading E. P. Thompson's *The Making of the English Working Class* by a pool at the University of California. It must have been near an air force base because my memory is of watching B-52 bombers taking off and lazily circling to cruising height, off on patrol, perhaps even to their failsafe points, should the balloon suddenly go up – which I thought ironic, given Thompson's role in the Campaign for Nuclear Disarmament.

Thompson's book – 958 pages of small, close-set type – was one that every serious left-wing historian of the time had to read but few did, the way every serious Christian one day plans to read the Old Testament, and every Young Liberal Ayn Rand's *The Fountainhead*. As a book it was so intellectually overwhelming that one needed a gap year to take it on, which is what I now had. I had spent the previous half-year since completing my BA doing shift work in various canning and assembly factories to save for the trip, so in important ways I was in the mood for Thompson's message about how the working-class communities that reached their zenith in places like Dandenong and Doveton created themselves out of the violence of the Industrial Revolution.

For reasons that will become obvious, Thompson's thesis is worth recounting briefly. At the end of the eighteenth century, the English working class of handloom weavers, agricultural labourers, ironworkers, miners and the like still lived a largely rural existence, employed at home or in small workshops, with strong connections to village or parish life. Yet by the early 1830s many had been agglomerated into large factories under the discipline of the overseer and the mechanical clock, and their once middling towns like Manchester, Liverpool and Leeds had been transformed into the 'dark satanic mills' of Blake's poem, with thousands upon thousands of factory hands crammed into dangerous slums, where they died young and poor. The old world had been physically transformed: bricked over, blackened, cheapened, uglified.

In the long run and on average, Britons ended up wealthier, the economists tell us, but the economic transformation was carried through with callousness and violence, according to a set of economic ideas imposed from on high, totally unrelieved by any sense of participation in a common project for the national good. Its ideology, according to Thompson, was that of the masters and the masters alone. In barely thirty years – the same period of time that spans from the mid-1980s to today – an economy that had previously served the whole community now served a narrow class of winners, practically enslaving the rest. It wasn't until the political system caught up half a century later that the material benefits began to be spread with any degree of justice. Thompson's book suggests a question: did it have to be done that way? This, in some ways, is our question too.

It's not surprising that people resisted this change, sometimes violently, by smashing up the power looms and threshing machines that had taken their jobs, and by forming unions, some of whose members were transported to Australia for their troubles. We have too easily forgotten that the horrors of the industrial revolution – the fourteen-hour days, the pregnant women down mines, the stunted children up chimneys, the life of hunger followed by an early death – existed in the folk memory of Australia's working-class settlers. (The same nightmare still haunts trade union officials whenever they hear the term 'WorkChoices'.) These horrors are what many early settlers came here to escape. Their idea of Australia was a society that worked for everyone, not just mine owners and factory owners and landholders. After crossing the Atlantic on my backpacking trip in

1985 I went to the Belfast streets where my parents grew up; I saw the cramped, dark flat in which they lived when they were first married and immediately understood why they had got on a ship to Australia and never gone back. In Doveton, life was stupendously better.

Something similar to E. P. Thompson's story of England in the first three decades of the 1800s has happened in Australia between the mid-1980s and today. Not the immiserisation (obviously, thanks to the victories of social democracy over the last century in creating a welfare state, there is no equivalent to the mass destitution of that time), but the pace and scale of social and economic change. The transformation from the industrial to the post-industrial era has been so total as to constitute the sociological equivalent of an extinction event.

The queues of workers' cars lining up to get into the factories – gone. The publicly owned banks and utilities – gone, or about to go. The union movement, which once covered half the employed workforce and rivalled the state for economic power – mostly gone (it's down now to just 12 per cent coverage in the private sector, replaced in part by the welfare lobby, which has had to step into the breach to speak up for the working poor). Secure, full-time employment, with its guarantee of holidays, sick pay and promotion – in many industries long gone.

And along with these changes to the world of work, the expectations of equal chances in life are also gone for many. The dream of home-ownership for all – gone. The levelling idea of the public school, attended by the children of factory manager and factory worker alike – gone. The easy-to-get apprenticeships that enabled young working-class Australians to get a toehold in the economy – gone. The hope of natural advancement through a firm, backed by in-house training – gone. Just as England's green and pleasant fields were paved over with brick, its vocations replaced by the machine, its pastoral life rent asunder by industrialisation, in just thirty years our little world, with its factories and the communities they supported, has been made extinct, wiped out like the dinosaurs by Professor Schumpeter's fiery asteroid. By a revolution.

The big problem for the creative destroyers is that the political, social and economic values of the Australian people were formed during the long post-war era of success, before the factories and the factory communities began to be smashed up. Australians still want their country to make things, still want laws that limit the boss's prerogatives, still want business and the better-off to pay a decent share of taxation, still want more training for their children, and still want a decent social safety net and universal health and education services. This egalitarian and nation-building outlook, which was formed in the post-war period of economic and social success, is the essence of the Australian national consciousness. It is the opposite of what the economic theorists want to impose upon us, and it is the thing that pulls them up every time they overreach. It is only because the Hawke and Keating governments tempered their creative destruction with imaginative and egalitarian social policy that they got as far as they did – and still, by the end, the electorate was waiting for them with its baseball bats. John Hewson ignored egalitarianism completely and failed completely. John Howard kept within eyesight of egalitarian sentiment for a while, but then tried to give Australia WorkChoices. Creative destruction is nothing if not unpopular.

Time and again the economic narrators smugly remind us of the scale of their revolutionary achievement. But they never tell the whole story. Between 1983 and 2015, Australia experienced a social and economic revolution as profound as any in our history; contrary to what they tell us, it has not all been for the good, and it could have been done differently. Those from working-class communities who have failed to gain a higher education, start a business or become successfully self-employed have lost a great deal, even when their take-home pay has increased. As E. P. Thompson put it, writing about the Industrial Revolution: 'People may consume more goods and become less happy and less free at the same time.' Understanding this fact is essential if we are to build a future that works for everyone.

My sister's old workmate from Heinz, Cheryl, articulated this better than anyone else could. Her working life – and, hence, her life – *was* better before the old economy was wiped out, and no MBA-toting economics adviser can tell her otherwise. And her example is representative of what has happened to hundreds of thousands, if not millions of other working-class Australians.

The national secretary of the National Union of Workers, Tim Kennedy, tells me he has another way of representing this. At gatherings of warehouse workers just like Cheryl (it's in warehousing that many former manufacturing workers now work – my other sister, Pamela, being another), he asks employees to line up from youngest to oldest, and asks how many started their working lives as permanent, full-time employees. Only the oldest workers put up their hands. Then he asks how many started with a full-time job. Those over forty years then put up their hands. Then he asks how many started as casuals. Almost everyone under forty then raises their hands.

Plot that on a graph if you must, because it tells you something. These workers' frustration is obvious. Those who work for major companies are proud to do so and have great loyalty to their firms, partly because they know that direct employment means they will be comparatively well looked after. But those employed indirectly through labour-hire firms, with no direct contractual relationship to the people whose imported products they move from one place to another, are far from happy about it, apart from their relief at having any sort of job at all. Under such arrangements, two-way loyalty is impossible.

It's not unusual, Kennedy says, for warehousing work-forces to be 60 per cent casual, 40 per cent permanent. Back at Heinz it was 100 per cent permanent, with casuals only being employed for seasonal work – an arrangement dictated by the logic of nature, not the logic of share-holder interests. And, he estimates, on the many current warehouse sites that once were factories, for every ten old factory workers there is barely one or two storemen or storewomen. Their jobs have gone, their work has inten-sified, they are not listened to, they are treated with less respect than their forebears, and managements are more ruthless and more tyrannical. Overall, their lives have become nastier and more brutal.

The economic reformers know this, of course; turning the nation's economy into the equivalent of a giant vac-uum cleaner that sucks all the wealth and power to the top is the whole point. They don't call it exploitation; they just phrase it differently: it is 'increased productivity'.

In his 2003 novel *Millennium People*, J. G. Ballard paints a picture of an England in which the professional middle class – de-unionised, largely self-employed, having to work all hours of the day instead of nine to five, totally at the whim of managers, enslaved to mortgages and private school fees, and suffering debilitating and soul-destroying anxieties as a result – is the new proletariat. In the neigh-bourhood of Chelsea Marina, its members form a new revolutionary class and begin a doomed revolt.

It's an intriguing concept that doesn't quite come off;

Millennium People is far from Ballard's best book. But it did kick-start a train of thinking that is now, more than a decade after the book's publication, becoming widespread: the idea that while the new economy may have made us wealthier (on average, at least), it hasn't made us happier, and that we're left wanting something more, even if we find it difficult to define exactly what that is.

The reason Ballard's story of middle-class revolt fails is because his obsession with middle-class dystopia blinds him to the real truth about the new economy. In the new economy the true exploited proletariat is not the new middle class, it is the new working class – which is to say the old one, although robbed of its power, freedom and affluence. The new proletariat is made up of the millions of people just like Cheryl. And it is only the anger of these millions of Cheryls, expressed through the ballot box, that stops state and federal governments from taking economic reform to its absolute extreme. They are the ones who are keeping the productivity commissioners and CEO class in check. If our revolution has heroes, here they are.

So why won't all those little people just lie down and let history trample over them? Why can't they see that all this economic reform has been for the best? Why don't they cheer when the economists remove public support for their industries and close down their factories and make them and their children unemployed? How can they be so ungrateful as not to thank Paul Keating for liberating them from their dull, monotonous, supposedly unskilled and unimportant jobs making cars? Can't they read the statistics? Can't they see the upward trends in per-capita GDP that come from liberalised markets? Are they blind to the cheaper price tags on imported goods? Don't they realise their children will thank them for sacrificing everything they have and know? Are they stupid?

There is nothing new about these questions. The issue of whether working-class living standards went up or down between 1800 and 1830 is one of the great historical debates, and it is still being fought. The grandfather of all economic reform, Friedrich von Hayek, wrote about it, which is why right-wing think tanks here in Australia still prosecute the 'yes' case in this 200-year-old dispute with such extraordinary enthusiasm. If the little people came out of the Industrial Revolution better off, the economic reformers contend, they will come out of our current de-industrial revolution better off too. E. P. Thompson's book leads the 'no' case, believing that the little people were morally right to resist.

In Australia today, the greatest insult any economist can hurl at you, perhaps apart from 'rent-seeker', is 'Luddite', which refers to the nineteenth-century English clothing workers who fought against the introduction of the steam-powered weaving machinery that turned them from respected artisans into unskilled, low-paid factory workers. (In fact, on the morning I wrote this passage the term appeared prominently in the *Australian Financial*

Review – in the column of a former Labor leader, no less.) Knowing what we now know about the comparative riches the economy had in store for these workers fifty years into the future, the 'yes' case argues, they should have folded – taken it on the chin for the nation, so to speak.

It is, of course, obvious to anyone except the creative destroyers that this view has a serious flaw: it is totally lacking in moral content. Humans don't work this way. They don't give up without a fight, they don't voluntarily accept poverty, and they don't surrender their culture and traditions without a struggle. The creative destroyers, with their high salaries and indexed pensions and share portfolios and property values to protect, are asking working Australians to make sacrifices for the common good which they themselves would never contemplate. The English working class actually went backwards materially for three decades and more: their working hours increased, their diets deteriorated, they became addicted to gin, and their children, crammed into slums and deprived of fresh air and clean water, died in greater numbers than before. More than this, the *quality* of their lives deteriorated too, by which is meant their way of life, their culture and their communities.

As Thompson famously put it, we have to rescue the people who fought against economic reform from 'the enormous condescension of posterity'. Their cause – which amounted to saving their own lives – may appear backward to us, and borderline criminal to economists, but that's not how it appeared to them at the time.

> Their aspirations were valid in terms of their own experience; and, if they were casualties of history, they remain, condemned in their own lives, as casualties. Our only criterion of judgement should not be whether or not a man's actions are justified in the light of subsequent evolution. After all, we are not at the end of social evolution ourselves. In some of the lost causes of the people of the Industrial Revolution we may discover insights into social evils which we have yet to cure.

And that's the point: just like the English working class who went through the Industrial Revolution, the people who experienced the destruction of places like Doveton have something important to say to us.

Every revolution needs a revolutionary class, and this one is no exception. It was carried through by the true heirs of the political psychology that once belonged to the Marxist Left: the economic reformers, armed with their philosophy of creative destruction, which Schumpeter stole from Marx.

When I call these people the heirs of the revolutionary psychology of Marxism, in many cases I mean it quite literally. We can place the beginnings of this revolution back in the late 1970s and early 1980s, when the ideologies of neoliberalism and neoconservatism, as implemented by the governments of Margaret Thatcher and Ronald Reagan, began to influence those Australian conservatives dismayed by the lack of reforming zeal of the government of Malcolm Fraser. Some of these intellectuals – the most notable being the then editor of the *Australian Financial Review*, P. P. McGuinness, who once worked for the Brezhnev-era Moscow Narodny Bank – were actual former pseudo-Marxist left-wing fellow travellers. Another node of this thinking, *Quadrant* magazine, contained similar characters who had moved from left to right over the course of their lives.

Like all revolutionary ideologies, this one began with a concept of freedom and a Promethean quest to transform the nation. Its historical task was to unleash the power of the market, which it saw as having been placed in chains by the overly powerful post-war state. And like all revolutionary ideologies, it believed that its central conviction – in this case, that the market should be totally free – was so important that it displaced other moral considerations. Just as in Marxist thought all social relations, institutions and rights had to give way to the logic of history, for the economic reformers all things had to give way to the logic of the market. The market had the right to destroy any social relations, from subsidised industry to trade unions to the local public school, because the market relations that replaced them would by their very nature create something better. With the help of neoconservatism, economic reform even developed its own pseudo-Marxist sociological terminology to justify all this – phrases like 'new class elite', 'provider capture' and 'rent-seeker' – and its own populist political strategy, which was to ignite a revolt by the people against the shadowy 'elites', which were somehow pulling the levers of power even when out of government.

In the face of this idea, which was carried through with such conviction that it even began to influence sizeable chunks of the Labor Party, communities like Doveton, whose economic strength lay in the partial subordination of the market to the needs of society, didn't stand a chance. The idea received a massive boost when federal treasurer Paul Keating induced a panic with his exaggerated claim in 1986 that Australia was done for and on the road to becoming a banana republic. The predictable end point was that people in places like Doveton would eventually be denounced as scroungers who, because they relied on transparent public support to keep their industries strong, were stealing wealth earned by others through the operations of the free market.

Equally predictably, though, was something else important: that this new ideology of freedom for the market, like all such revolutionary ideologies, would calcify into a formula that would in fact narrow the way we see the world, limit our imaginations, take away our ability to think in moral terms and reduce our capacity to conceive of something better. Creative destruction has become an intellectual straightjacket, like Marxism became in Eastern Europe. And this calcification is exactly what has happened here in Australia. It was carried through by the managerialists, the *nomenklatura* of the neoliberal age.

On the death of Robin Williams, a friend of mine, Emily, sent me a link to a YouTube clip of the best scene from *Dead Poets Society*. I am what you would call very pro-Williams – many people aren't – and mainly because of this movie, which I saw with a girlfriend I was very fond of when it was released in 1989. At twenty-five and about to head off to Cambridge, I was still young enough to put myself in the shoes of the movie's students; arriving there still infected by Peter Weir's great story, in which the heroes are the romantic poets Whitman, Thoreau, Byron and Tennyson, I was determined not to spend all my time conducting some dry-as-dust academic research but to be the sort of student the Williams character – who was named (for us perhaps ironically) Mr Keating – would have wanted me to be. I would try to read everything – the classics, philosophy, literature, poetry – and breathe deeply the romance of the great university town. My PhD thesis would be a meal ticket and no more. If I didn't fully succeed in this, I did at least try.

I'm now older than Mr Keating was in the film, and seeing the YouTube clip affected me in a different way. The teacher's message still seemed subversive, but for different reasons. You may recall the scene. Mr Keating, who has just taken the job of English master at the exclusive male boarding school where he himself was once a student, asks his class to open their poetry textbook, written by one Dr J. Evans Pritchard, at the introduction. He tells one student, Neil, to read the opening paragraph. It says that the greatness of a poem can be determined in a relatively simple way, by gauging first how artfully the objective of the poem has been rendered (through the use of meter, rhyme and figures of speech) and then how important that objective is. And the simplest way to do this is to plot these qualities on a graph, with the poem's artistic perfection ('P') plotted horizontally and its importance ('I') plotted vertically: 'Calculating the total area of the poem yields the measure of its greatness.' As Neil is reading this, Mr Keating draws such a graph on the blackboard, and next to it the formula 'P × I = G'. He then turns to the class and says, 'Excrement!' before instructing his pupils to take Dr J. Evans Pritchard's introductory chapter in their hands and 'Rip it out!'

In 1989 the culture wars were just beginning, and this scene became one of its early battles. It fitted the template perfectly: Keating's instruction to his class to rip out the text as a metaphor for the corrupting of the young, who were being incited by their irresponsible teachers to reject authority and take up a romantic variant of nihilism. Writing in 1990, the Australian sociologist John Carroll – whose work I admire, even though I suspect our political views might be diametrically opposed – shrewdly observed in an essay in Robert Manne's *Quadrant* that although *Dead Poets Society* is set in 1959, it is 'the most persuasive presentation of 1960s ideology there has ever been'. To Carroll, the 1960s, far from being unique, was a ritual playing out of the sort of romantic revolt that periodically convulses the West 'every time the middle-class order, stipulated on family, vocation, duty and civil society, swings into its own decadence ruled by snobbery and greed', the French Revolution and the Romantic movement being the most recent cases. From this perspective, Carroll continues, *Dead Poets Society* 'is evidence that a new bout of profane materialism has indeed emerged in the 1980s'.

I think Carroll is on to something important, although his political target is the wrong one. To Carroll, ripping out the introduction to the poetry textbook, with its reassuring sense of order triumphing over romantic rebellion, was an act of mindless, anti-intellectual destruction. But to me, removing its philistine formulas seems the first step towards understanding poetry's true meaning, and by extension the true meaning of any intellectual endeavour. In the field of public policy, if human feeling cannot trump mathematical calculation, we are in danger of becoming a mere economy rather than a society, digits on some economist's spreadsheet rather than human beings living in actual communities.

Exhibit one for this position also came to me from

Emily. Recently, attending a policy seminar put on by one of Australia's better-funded think tanks, she was shown a PowerPoint graph titled 'Figure A.1: Framework for prioritising economic reform'. In the same way Dr J. Evans Pritchard asks students to plot the greatness of Byron's odes and Shakespeare's sonnets on a graph, the think-tank asks us to determine the greatness of policy ideas two-dimensionally. On the vertical axis, one plots the estimated additional gross domestic product in the year 2022 created by any proposed reform. And on the horizontal, one plots the degree of confidence we have that the government can intervene successfully to achieve the expected gains. In shorthand, we might write something like: *Expected GDP × Confidence of Success = A Better World*, or GDP × C = B.

In the spirit of Mr Keating, we might say, for instance, that a reform like the Rudd/Gillard mining tax might score high on the vertical but low on the horizontal, and therefore is not worth contemplating. But a tax reform to reward savings by superannuants might score high both horizontally and vertically, yielding a massive total area and therefore revealing the reform to be truly great (even if also highly regressive). Also following Mr Keating, we might respond with a single word: 'Excrement.'

The most worrying thing about this graph is that it actually does represent how many of our policymakers think and talk. It's a sort of Zen representation of the policy world: on the one axis GDP, on the other political calculation. But where are the people? Isn't reform supposed to be about them? Their absence explains all you need to know. If the little people won't accept economic reform, it's because when they hear policymakers argue for reform using reasoning like this, they know their interests don't count. They are right to reject it.

It's easy, especially for those on the Left, to blame neoliberalism. The people may very well be rejecting neoliberal economic reform, but the issue is actually a broader one that is shared by all political parties in Australia: the democratic inadequacy of managerialism. Economic reform may have started out as a political philosophy of freedom in the courts of Thatcher and Reagan, but it has hardened into a process formulated by Australia's managerial class across all parties, and led intellectually by the theorists who inspire the great management consultancy firms.

Twenty years of being up-close to policymakers has convinced me that many have been wholly captured by the concerns and methodologies of the management consulting industry. McKinsey, Bain, Boston and so on have become the training grounds for the new policy elite of economists and other assorted 'wonks', who, wielding their favoured weapons of the spreadsheet and the PowerPoint deck, now inhabit the ministerial offices, policy units, departmental policy taskforces, think-tanks, industry associations and lobby groups that together determine what goes before parliament in the budget and in the most important social legislation.

The Productivity Commission functions as the Great Sanhedrin at the head of this new totalising economic reform religion. Its priorities are only those that can be represented by the use of data, and its idol is that elusive and occasionally nonsensical construct 'productivity'. And the language in which its priorities and schemes are expressed is abstract, symbolic, often indecipherable and invariably devoid of the one quality that separates people from computer processors: human feeling. As in *Dead Poets Society*, there is no room in its reasoning for the poetry of human feelings, just maths.

It's hardly an exaggeration to say that productivity has become *the* guiding principle of government in Australia today. Of the three Ps emphasised by the *Intergenerational Report* (the nation's premier long-term planning statement), productivity clearly outstrips participation and population in the centrality of its importance. This obsession – for that is what it is – was started by the Coalition, which set up the Productivity Commission in 1998, but has been advanced with some fervour by Labor, most noticeably the Rudd government. Looking to head off criticisms that its reforms were too statist and anti-market, but at the same time not wanting to appear neo-liberal, Labor policymakers got into the habit of defending their reforms not on moral or free-market grounds but on the grounds that they lifted national productivity.

Take education. When the Rudd government was first elected, education was arguably its most important policy area. Rudd promised us nothing less than an 'Education Revolution'. Here is how the special Education Revolution statement in that government's first budget opened: 'Investing in education is crucial to driving productivity growth and to building a modern and prosperous economy for the future.' As an opening statement, it was revealing indeed of the government's real priority. Not education. Not the nobility of learning or the ideal of transmitting knowledge to the young. Not even the social-democratic idea of promoting equality. In fact, the true priority did not relate to anything inherent in the idea of education itself. No, it was all about productivity.

As a speechwriter employed by numerous federal departments between 2007 and 2013, I witnessed this unfold day by day. Almost every speech draft I worked on would come back with the same instructions. 'Please,' it would ask, 'add in Krugman's line about productivity.' If you don't know it, here it is (although having been commanded to write it so many times, I find it almost painful): 'Productivity isn't everything, but in the long run it is almost everything.' Because it came from Krugman, a Nobel Prize winner and a grand man of the Left, the sentence had been elevated to the status of an unquestionable maxim, like 'what goes up must come down'. But question it for yourself. 'Productivity is almost everything?' Being thus qualified – 'almost' – it sounds so reasonable, doesn't it? I say no, on two counts.

The first is that the concept itself is largely a definitional nightmare and, ultimately, a statistical nonsense. It seems simple enough at first. The most commonly used productivity measure, 'multifactor productivity', measures the efficiency with which an economy converts inputs (given amounts of labour and capital) into outputs (goods and services). But it's not actually that simple. For a start, determining the level of productivity at any one time relies on estimates of inputs and outputs whose accuracy is often highly uncertain. Then there is the problem of determining what causes productivity to go up or down. Are rises in productivity produced mainly by technological advances, as the Left prefers to think, or by microeconomic reform which sweeps away inefficiencies and squeezes more from the workforce, as the Right argues? No one can say – it's purely a matter of your political point of view.

Then there are the paradoxes produced by the fact that productivity is a ratio involving continually changing variables. So, for instance, productivity can fall when investment in new plant and equipment increases (as it did during the mining boom, when our economic growth was the envy of the world), and it can fall when higher numbers of people are employed to produce more things (as it did during the great boom years of the 1960s). When unemployment increases, so can productivity if output remains stable or goes up. And when employment increases, productivity can go down unless output increases by more. It's easy to see, therefore, how productivity can trump full employment as a national objective, even though the latter has greater moral worth and popular support.

Productivity can also fall when we regulate for a cleaner environment and produce boutique 'artisanal' products of higher quality that people want to buy (like hand-crafted beer); conversely, it can rise when we pollute our air and drink tasteless generic lager. As I have mentioned, because productivity is essentially a ratio, these sorts of paradoxes are to be expected, but this can lead to absurd situations – including the ultimate absurdity whereby our economy can produce less with a much higher rate of unemployment and still see productivity go up.

So it's possible for a nation to be poorer and more productive at the same time. It shouldn't come as any surprise, therefore, that Australia has managed to come out of thirty years of economic reform with higher productivity but still have places like Doveton, where unemployment is through the roof and many people are unable to produce anything at all. It wouldn't surprise me if the productivity of the Doveton economy has gone up even as its neighbourhoods lie in ruins – in fact, it would make perfect sense. The fact is that productivity has limited use as a guide to what we should do as a nation because it is devoid of all moral content.

Given all this, it's no wonder that even the Productivity Commission itself can't agree on exactly how the concept should be measured – and if it can't be certain, how can we? Certainly the general idea of economic efficiency has its logical attractions, but to propose widespread economic change solely on the basis of a concept as impossible to define and measure as productivity is the height of insanity.

The second count against productivity is that there are so many priorities of government – even so many *economic* priorities of government – that, far from being 'everything' or 'almost everything', productivity is, arguably, almost nothing. Let's set aside the thousands of legal, administrative and technical things we expect governments to do in our name and consider only the numerous economic ones. We expect governments to raise revenue and manage the nation's finances responsibly; to raise loans in order to finance investment, and to pay them back; to ensure that our schools and hospitals and other services are well funded; to stop bridges from collapsing, roads from developing pot holes and ports from rotting into the waves; to reduce the extremes of poverty and wealth through progressive taxation and a sound welfare system; to keep an eye on the balance of trade and stop it from ballooning in either direction; to prevent recessions; to keep interest rates at optimal levels; to keep inflation in check; to keep unemployment down; to stop the currency from getting too high or too low; and so forth. And yet so many of our economists think that everything must come second to continuing economic reform, as measured by the statistical phantom of productivity increase. It all reminds you of a cricket coach so lost in the data spewing out of his computer that he forgets that the idea is to win the game by scoring more runs than the other team.

One might argue that, in the pursuit of rising productivity, we sometimes stuff everything else up; numerous highly productive American cities with competitive business taxes and low minimum wages but bankrupt budgets, crumbling infrastructure and mass poverty can attest to that. Does this mean that raising productivity isn't an important goal of government policy? Of course not. Efficiency has its place. Within selected government departments there could usefully be units working on strategies to make our nation more productive in various ways, but even within the Department of Treasury this should be a boutique task in comparison with the core jobs of managing the nation's finances, creating jobs, fighting inflation and so forth. To judge everything else – fiscal policy, employment policy, living standards and social equality – according to what it means for productivity is folly. And for a party like the ALP to reduce its social-democratic quest to the morally and emotionally empty goal of raising productivity is the slow road to political suicide. People will follow Labor to the barricades in defence of the ideal of equality, but not for the productivity ratio.

There is no surer sign of the weakness of this managerialist approach to politics than that it has already hardened into a template. Examine almost any major policy idea these days – it might be designed to improve the performance of early childhood education, schools, universities, hospitals, rail transport, freight delivery or a dozen other things – and you will find a similar formula. Announce a national goal of achieving universal access to a certain minimum standard; set new performance targets; establish a framework against which to measure service standards; define the sort of data that would be useful to achieving this; introduce a data-gathering process; publish the data on a public website to put pressure on the service deliverers and create a market with perfect information; link this data, perhaps in the form of statistically modified league tables, to new pools of quality-assurance funding to correct failure; and, finally, set up peer-to-peer information sharing among the relevant professions to drive continuous learning.

This sort of thing, bought off the shelf from the large management consulting firms, seldom works. The data may get collected and published, eventually, but the necessary funding to make it all work and achieve the promised results never seems to appear. The Gonski school reforms are the greatest and saddest example of this, but far from the only ones. It's managerial fantasy by formula, and only serves to stop politicians from thinking about what they should really be doing.

If you watch our politicians talk about reform policies like these, you seldom hear simple statements of common logic, belief, ideology, philosophy, morality or even emotion. All you hear is them flipping over in their minds the PowerPoint slides the consulting firms have devised using the logic, symbols and priorities of managerialism. The following fictional exchange would be typical:

> INTERVIEWER: Minister, your policy isn't working, is it?
>
> MINISTER: That's not correct. The goals have been set. Our Quality Standards Framework is in place. Crucial data has been gathered and is about to be published ...
>
> INTERVIEWER: But you've just announced that early targets have not been met – in fact results are going backwards. Your flagship funding program has been radically scaled back, promised training programs to build the new workforce have not eventuated ...
>
> MINISTER: That's because the states and territories won't cooperate ...

You know the rest. Devising policy like this makes perfect sense to the managerialists in charge of our reform processes, but the people can see through it. And that's why they are switching off in large numbers and seeking answers beyond the major parties.

Let's think about what the managerialists have done to our language. This is an easy target, admittedly; lampooning managerialist sludge has itself descended into cliché, and I won't do it here. It suffices to say that when policymakers talk about 'inputs', 'interventions' and 'outcomes', and especially about 'productivity', they're not talking about real changes to the way we live. They're talking about the symbols, abstractions and data they use to measure and represent the results of these changes. It's a new language that is altogether different from the one ordinary people speak: words become numbers, verbs become processes, poetry becomes two-dimensional and prose becomes PowerPoint. It's dull and alienating, obviously, but it does more than simply damage a government's ability to communicate with the people (which in a democracy is serious enough); it also stops a government from having any true purpose at all.

Recently, nearing the end of an election campaign, I heard a party leader answer a question about what sort of government there would be should he win by saying it would be 'a government focused on outcomes'. To any political leader, this sort of thing makes a rough sense, being shorthand for 'we won't be ideological or extreme but moderate, sensible and middle-of-the-road, and we will keep our promises', or some other variety of blandness. But to the rest of us it is meaningless. In this case it was proof that the prospective new government's priorities would be little more than those the management consultants could redefine, measure and tick off. Hospital waiting lists down – tick. Suburban train delays down – tick. Spending on school maintenance up – tick. And so forth, all while horror stories about postponed operations, late trains and demountable classrooms continue.

Dependent on their policy advisers, such politicians are like the prisoners chained to the wall of Plato's metaphorical cave: they see and hear only abstract representations and echoes of political, economic and social reality. From the perspective of the policymakers – who have never left their caves, never spent much time in places like

Doveton and therefore have never seen what effect their ideas have on the lives of actual people and communities – their formulas and ideas are unquestionable, the height of wisdom itself, and opposing them seems completely irrational. If we just get rid of the minimum wage and penalty rates to make workplaces more flexible (or put a 'price signal' on visiting a doctor and extend the GST to cover food, or let the market determine the level of university fees, or test every school student and put the results on a website, or get rid of subsidies to manufacturing and buy our vehicles and submarines and processed food from other countries, or remove the restrictions on the importation of foreign labour), then we will attain rising levels of economic productivity, win the praise of Paul Kelly, be compared to Paul Keating, have a graph that rates high on both the vertical and the horizontal axes simultaneously, and be considered truly great.

There is only one way to proceed: we must heed Robin Williams' call, take the 'Framework for prioritising economic reform' and *rip it out.*

To understand what's really going on in our economy and our society, we need a better language than the one on offer from the managerialists, one that tells us the truth but hasn't had the important elements of human feeling sucked out of it. It wouldn't hurt occasionally to listen to artists.

In literature, the past is usually one great eternal summer. To George Orwell, writing between his mid-thirties to mid-forties (roughly 1939 to 1949), childhood represented not just carefree youth but a past that he was certain was superior to the present. Yes, it included coal miners coughing their lungs up in rain-swept northern villages, men doffing their caps in the presence of the landlord or the boss, and the thin red line protecting the opium monopoly in some far-flung colony. But the countryside had not yet been overrun by suburbia – Orwell's detested 'villa-civilisation' – with its motorways and faux Tudor pubs. Sturdy carthorses grazed in open fields; dace still swam in unpolluted streams and ponds; beer still tasted like beer; the Great War hadn't killed a million Englishmen; the Great Depression hadn't reduced the working class to starving beggars; totalitarianism, with its propaganda and surveillance, hadn't been thought of; and the Luftwaffe hadn't turned London into a rubble heap. The things we now consider unquestionable benefits of scientific and technical progress – which prolong our lives, keep us warm in winter and cool in summer, and allow us to travel the world for a few thousand dollars – had not yet arrived, meaning that, to the majority, the idea of 'progress' was largely theoretical, a swindle, a bringer of mass destruction. Looked at in this way, Orwell had a point. He called this memory of the past 'the Golden Country', and it is central to the meaning of his best novels, *Coming Up for Air* (1939), *Animal Farm* (1946) and *Nineteen Eighty-Four* (1949).

Orwell, of course, isn't the only writer to notice that progress comes with a cost, and that the march of time doesn't necessarily make life better. Two of my favourite novels, L. P. Hartley's *The Go-Between* and J. L. Carr's *A Month in the Country*, also deal with this idea: men returning to the places of their youth, where the formative events of their lives took place. Why is the superiority of the past such a recurrent theme of literature? It's a form of pastoral, of course, and thus nostalgia, not meant to be taken literally. But does the appeal of the past lie only in the fact that the past was when we were younger and more carefree, fitter and stronger, without mortgages to pay and superannuation balances to worry about, and had possibly fallen in love for the first time? Maybe. But could it be that, in some essential ways, the past *was* better? Could it be that, as Shelley once observed, it is actually great artists (and not, we might add, economists and change-management theorists) who are most sensitive to the transformations going on around us, who best understand what those changes have in store and whether they really do add up to something superior, and who are best placed to tell us how to proceed?

If this is so, then pastoral has something to tell us, because in all pastoral, as in the paintings of Poussin, beneath the drooping vines and beyond the prancing minstrels, there lies a truth of sorts: that life, in many of its important and easily definable aspects, actually *was* better once. When, in their dismissive way, economists tell us to forget the past and embrace a risky new world, we should not necessarily acquiesce, at least not fully or without a fight. Ordinary people – and by this I don't mean 'change agents' – understand this, and this is why change is often resisted, and why opposition to change will always find a listening ear.

Asked to come up with a theme for a major lecture to be given by one of my speechwriting clients, the then Labor treasurer, Wayne Swan, I encouraged him to talk about something he knew and loved: the poet of blue-collar America, Bruce Springsteen. The speech made the point that artistic sensibility is much like the finely sprung workings of a seismometer, sensing motions deep beneath the surface of society, the first rumblings of change. Economists can do that, admittedly, with their repetitive predictions about how the global free market is coming to destroy everything, and that the best we can do is hasten its triumph by shutting our mouths and surrendering – freedom being nothing more to them than the recognition of necessity. But their chants are less like warnings than commands. This is because economics, unlike art, lacks a serious moral dimension. Data, after all, doesn't 'do' morality, being incapable of telling us what economic and social change means for the quality of our lives, beyond how much GDP it might, theoretically, create for some of us. If, for example, the data tells us that greater inequality will produce higher GDP, then many managerialists, including some normally quite left-wing ones, will accept it as necessary for the national good. I wouldn't. Springsteen's songs, by contrast, amplified echoes of the decline of blue-collar affluence, quality of life and happiness in America that Springsteen had heard in his New Jersey home town, the sort of place the dismal scientists ignorantly or wilfully never see, and whose decline they can only conceive as a good thing.

The problem this analysis faces is our inability to recall what this quite recent past, this life before the economic transformations of the mid-1980s, was like. It may have sounded like a Bruce Springsteen rock ballad from *Darkness on the Edge of Town*, or maybe some song written for Cold Chisel by Don Walker – 'Flame Trees', perhaps. But what did it *look* like? It is too easy for the boosters of economic reform to dismiss this past as always overcast and raining, brown-walled and acrylic-carpeted, greasy-haired, cigarette-smoking, pallid and poor. If you look hard, though, you can still catch glimpses of how this past moved and worked.

I have before me a magazine called *International Auge of Mexico*. It's a massive, magnificent, glossy representation of the world before the internet. *Auge* translates roughly as 'peak' or 'apogee', and every edition was a separate feature on countries or places then considered on the rise. This one is a special edition from April 1973 all about Australia, called *Australia the Awakening Giant*. Going by what the creative destroyers tell us, we should expect to see a portrait of a drab, dreary, bogan country, a place in decline as it is slowly strangled by corporatism, tottering on its wobbly forelegs like an obese heifer, waiting for the Yom Kippur War, the Arab oil embargo and Vietnam-linked inflation to finish it off. Instead, Australia is portrayed as full of life and potential. Australia was once cut off and largely unknown, the magazine says. 'But today, with rapid communication and transportation, Australia is neither unknown nor isolated, and has taken its proper place on the map as one of the most rapidly growing and progressive countries in the world.'

Off every page of the magazine leap bright pictures of thrusting skylines of modernist architecture, rapid transit systems, high-tech communications, cultural sophistication, leading-edge manufacturing industries with new factories producing 450,000 shiny new cars a year, radio-controlled pilotless aircraft and bulk container ships, all interposed with the more traditional representations of agriculture, the outback, Indigenous history and Australians at play on the beach. 'Australia's industrialisation,' it says, 'has come a long way in a short time; all the ingredients – resources, expertise, sound economy, population growth and stable government – are there for it to continue its dramatic story of development. So this is Australia,' it continues, 'a land quite unlike any other. It is a country well worth getting to know, not only because of its intrinsic fascination but also because it deserves to be recognised as a nation with a tremendous future.'

All up, Australia in April 1973 looks a pretty damn nice place to live. No wonder Australians over fifty remember it that way. To put it mildly, this is not the picture the economic reformers want us to see, because it contradicts their convenient story that, before they came along to rescue it, the Australian economy was lying face-down in the gutter.

The Hollywood epic *The Deer Hunter*, directed by Michael Cimino, is another piece of evidence, though far less glossy. Much criticised despite winning five Oscars, most of the movie, especially its orientalist representations of Asia, doesn't stand up today. However, the opening act, set around work, marriage, drinking and deer hunting in a Pittsburgh steel town, supposedly in 1967 but really in 1978, is like a time capsule of a way of life that barely exists today, except in folk memory and the grooves of Springsteen's early LPs. What is of interest is the representation of a world in which the working class, through its unions, its culture and the economic power that resided in its muscles, was still master of its own little world. Its culture is rough, male, lubricated by beer and bourbon chasers, and punctuated by periodic fistfights – so it is best not totally idealised. But because we now know what came after – deindustrialisation and economic devastation – we can see that something significant was lost with its passing. What was it?

This story of loss is told by the *New Yorker* writer George Packer in his book *The Unwinding: An Inner History of the New America*. As Packer tells it, in the wake of the Reagan revolution, de-industrialisation began to spread like a cancer along the highways of old blue-collar America, bringing with it unemployment, drugs and rising crime rates. In Ohio the steel plants downsized and then shut – or, rather, moved to Mexico, where the labour was cheaper (just like Heinz moved from Dandenong to New Zealand). Workers over fifty took their retirement and the younger ones left town; the owner-managed strip shops went under and were replaced by ugly, minimum-wage-paying low-cost chain stores like Wal-Mart, built on Springsteen's dark edge of town; houses lay empty and then were vandalised and burnt; whole neighbourhoods were depopulated and became ghost towns; local taxes dried up, decimating municipal police forces and allowing gangs to get a stranglehold over the streets; schools went into decline and student grades fell, taking away any hope of upward social mobility; and crack cocaine finally dissolved what was left, the way gin did in Hogarth's eighteenth-century England. Our picture of Doveton is starting to look familiar.

As Packer puts it:

> Over the years, America had become more like Wal-Mart. It had gotten cheap. Prices were lower, and wages were lower. There were fewer union factory jobs, and more part-time jobs as store greeters. The small towns where Mr. Sam [Wal-Mart's creator, Sam Walton] had seen his opportunity were getting poorer, which meant that consumers there depended more and more on everyday low prices, and made every last purchase at Wal-Mart, and maybe had to work there, too.

So ask yourself: if you were a blue-collar American, where and when would you have preferred to live: Michael Cimino's Pennsylvania or George Packer's Ohio? The world created by post-war planners and ruled over by industries and trade unions, or that created by modern market economists? And if you were a blue-collar Australian, in which Doveton would you want to live: the Doveton of then or the Doveton of now? We have improved on the past in many ways, and one could easily point to places in Australia where life is far better now, but not in Doveton and other murdered suburbs.

If, as L. P. Hartley wrote at the start of *The Go-Between*, 'The past is a foreign country: they do things differently there', then the past in Doveton was a different suburb. Its people were at the centre of things in a way they clearly are not now: they all had jobs. Their past was better than their present. But what of their future?

CHAPTER 5
HISTORY TO THE DEFEATED

Who controls the past controls the future:
who controls the present controls the past.
    —George Orwell

Let's begin our examination of the future by thinking about the thing that must make it better: the Australian Labor Party. Over the last thirty years Labor has lost its way amid the economic revolution it started and led for much of the time. Like a wild horse, that revolution has escaped from its handlers and is threatening the party's future. What must Labor do to find its way again?

A good place to start is to think about why people join the ALP in the first place. A while back I had lunch with a thirty-something Labor lawyer who revealed that, having joined the ALP just after her fifteenth birthday, she had recently resigned, dispirited at its failure to project sufficient idealism. Stories like this are commonplace, so rather than ask why she left, I was more interested to ask why she had joined at just fifteen, which is somewhat unusual.

'Well,' she said, 'it's part of the family's story.' When her grandfather, a docker, was killed just at the end of World War II, his former comrades, hardly well off themselves, sacrificed their spare shillings to a widow's fund that helped her grandmother to keep her nine children from hunger and cold.

That's why people once joined the ALP! Thanks to Australia's recent wealth spurt, few today live in fear of the penury that grandmother faced. My point is that while this Labor story involves economics, it isn't essentially an economic story, and one shouldn't answer it simply by emphasising modern Labor's economic credentials. It's a romantic moral tale, one that appeals to a radical spirit in Australian culture, and one that today's progressives, considering joining the Greens but not really wanting to, are crying out for Labor to tell anew. That grandmother's life may perhaps have been improved by a productivity ratio with a 2 in front of it – or maybe not, if it involved industrial-relations reform that threw her benefactors out of their jobs – but making the economy stronger isn't an end in itself; creating a better society is. In short, Labor has to remember that it is primarily a social movement, not a policy unit of the Department of Treasury.

Downplaying its own radical history would be a mistake for Labor as it seeks to build a viable future. To paraphrase Orwell, if Labor's managerialists control its past, the party may not have a future at all. Labor's thinkers should get writing. And one of the things they must do for a start is get over the Hawke and Keating era.

This may seem strange. After all, that duo is generally regarded as having presided over the most successful government the ALP has ever formed. My problem isn't that people continue to recognise and celebrate the successes of that period in office; it's that for too many in modern Labor, and the political class generally, Labor history doesn't seem to exist prior to 1983, the year the party began its reinvention as one of market-liberal economic reform.

This idea occurred to me a few years back, when a Gillard government speechwriter showed me a draft of a speech that contained a curious historical simile. Praising some new government initiative – I can't remember what it was – it said: 'This is our floating of the dollar.' Not our Snowy River Hydro Scheme or our Medicare; our *floating of the dollar*. The great nation-building achievements of Chifley and Whitlam had been replaced as Labor's 'Light on the Hill' by the deregulation of the currency. Since 1983, Labor's purpose, along with its history, has been turned on its head.

How has this happened? One obvious reason is that a number of ministers in the Rudd and Gillard governments once served in or worked for the Hawke and Keating governments, and they saw their job as completing its program. This is only natural – after all, it wasn't until the rise of Bill Clinton that the Democratic Party stopped trying to complete the New Deal. But I think there's another explanation: the extraordinary success of the Hawke/ Keating generation of ministers, advisers and senior press gallery figures in writing and selling the first – and, to date, unchallenged – draft of the history of their own era. The recent history of the modern ALP, and of Australia more generally, has largely been written by participants in the great economic reform crusade and their admirers. Their books take up at least half a shelf in my study. Not just Hawke and Keating themselves, but the former advisers and the commentators who took their economic reform program on as a cause, especially the *Australian*'s Paul Kelly with his (currently) three-volume *End of Certainty* thesis. Theirs was the era of the economist as hero, the neoliberal reformer as revolutionary, the big-picture man as patriot, the productivity ratio as the measure of national progress. Never, it seems, has a generation been so worthy and its vision so noble and unchallengeable.

So thorough has been their crafting of this new narrative that they have imprinted on the Labor psyche the belief that only those who take up and carry forward the dropped banner of managerialist 'economic reform' are worthy to be considered true national leaders. Hence the appeal to 'our floating of the dollar'; hence the feeling of *déjà vu* brought on by the 'new' big-picture narrative of the Asian century; hence the never-ending calls for more tariff cuts and more business tax cuts and more labour market reform and so on. Together, these storytellers have raised the philosophy and practice of the Hawke/

Keating governments to the status of a religion, and made the productivity ratio the measure of all things. Those who buck it by definition fall short.

This thesis is repeated time after time after time by a new generation of Labor historians and chroniclers. The towering genius of Hawke and Keating and the inability of Rudd and Gillard to match it is the central message of just about every book on the Labor Party published in the last half-dozen years. No countervailing story has yet to knock this narrative off its course.

This is not to denigrate the achievements of the 1980s and '90s generation in any way. Hawke and Keating did have a certain greatness, there's no doubting that. And their chroniclers and policy advisers are merely doing what every generation does, which is to project their achievement as the end of history. But here's the really big problem: history never ends. The Hawke government was elected thirty-two years ago, as I write. But the Berlin Wall fell more than a quarter of a century ago, 9/11 happened fourteen years ago, and the global financial crisis happened seven years ago. The world has changed, capitalism has changed, people's priorities change, and so social-democratic parties and their objectives must change too. The old agendas simply won't suffice. Labor has to stop listening to the critics who say it has diverged too far from the path of St Bob and St Paul, and start addressing the here and now, and the future.

Where are those answers to be found? That's easy: in

history, including the history of the Labor Party prior to 1983. As a speechwriter, one of my heroes is Cicero. In his book *Orator*, in which he sought to rouse Marcus Brutus to save the Republic from the chaos of the 40s, Cicero provided us with a line that should be every political historian's motto: 'To be ignorant of what happened before you were born is to remain forever a child.' Greatness requires deep historical knowledge, according to Cicero. You can't be insightful or persuasive if you don't have the ability to make comparisons with past events and eras. Lack of a broad historical perspective produces a moral shallowness, a narrowness of purpose and a crippling inability to inspire. Worst of all, it leaves you poorly equipped to respond to change. This, Cicero tells us, is the power of history. (And that, incidentally, is why speechwriters are invariably historians.)

Reforming the economy to lift productivity worked as a framing objective for Labor between 1983 and 1996, and no doubt it will remain an important tool of Labor governments in the years ahead, because, as I have mentioned earlier, efficiency and productivity are moderately important policy objectives, though much overrated. But productivity cannot remain the Labor Party's religion, and it cannot remain the sole measure of Labor's success. The Hawke/Keating mythologists are, in my view, the pied pipers of the ALP, leading the party into a deep and dark place, one lacking in moral purpose, from which it will be hard to find an exit. Labor's future success – and, potentially, its survival as the dominant party of the Left – lies in pursuing a much broader and more timeless objective. In short, it lies in rediscovering a moral and political language capable of appealing to a majority of its party members, supporters and voters. The managerialists' message won't suffice.

It all starts, I believe, with an effort to change the way we conceive and express our political and social problems. As I have stated, the economic reform ideology that brought on the great revolution of the last thirty years has hardened into a rigid formula that is robbing the ALP of its true purpose. And an overreliance on managerialist forms of reasoning has left us incapable of addressing the problems we face, causing our analysis to be channelled down narrow paths and our responses to be shallow and needlessly destructive.

We have become governed by the philosophy of the bulldozer, clearing the litter of human emotion, community cohesion and history from the path of economic reform, rather than considering how we can build on the past and ensure that economic change can be channelled to the benefit of society. So we need to enrich our thinking and our talk with insights from areas such as morality, history and aesthetics. By making a conscious effort to stop dismissing people's lives as 'outcomes', to avoid using tautological maxims like 'what gets measured gets improved', 'productivity is almost everything' and 'GDP × C = B', and to stop using unhelpful epithets like 'rent-seeker' and 'Luddite', we can begin to think and speak in ways that give us a chance of addressing the problems facing us. Five ways of thinking can aid this.

First, thinking morally. We have to recognise that losers matter, and that the losers from change have just as many rights as winners. Throughout history the cause of the underdog has generally been the morally superior one: Spartacus against the legions of Crassus, African slaves against cotton planters, the Tolpuddle Martyrs against the threshing machine, Ned Kelly against the colonial police, Bernie Banton against the mining giants. Until very recently in our history, this belief in the moral superiority of the underdog and the loser has been at the heart of our culture: witness Jimmy Barnes' 'Working Class Man'. Can we really say with any confidence that this type of sentiment dominates now, especially when millions of underdogs are being pulverised by a changing economy?

In the world of creative destruction, only the winners from change seem to matter and to have economic and social rights – it's as if the losers magically cease to exist, and the condemnation of whole suburbs to poverty for several generations is not a fit subject for moral judgment. The unproductive have only themselves to blame. We are urged to celebrate as 'lifters' the entrepreneurs whose technologies throw people out of work, and to condemn as 'leaners' those who have worked tirelessly and conscientiously for their employers, only to have the rug pulled from under them. With the redefinition of trade unionists as corrupt, rent-seeking scroungers, targeted by a royal commission, this process of redefining the working class as the economic enemy is now all but complete.

Why is this important? Because it is only by acknowledging the moral shortcomings of economic and social change that we might advance beyond the morality of the early 1800s. It might be remembered that the Labor Party itself – in fact, the social-democratic movement worldwide – was a movement created by the losers from the disruption of the late Industrial Revolution, and that those losers, acting together, managed to create a future that few would dispute has improved life for the overwhelming majority. It's from the losers that real change comes, not from comfortable winners, even if they're well-meaning do-gooders who think they can tweak the market to help the poor.

Second, thinking historically. We need to recognise that the past and the present have rights and should be respected. This, at first blush, seems a strange thing to say; after all, how can a period in time possibly have rights? It is not a living thing. So what do I mean by it? Simply this: that our policymakers have too few qualms about destroying the industries and communities the nation has built up over many years if an economist tells them that doing so will make us wealthier in the future. If productivity demands it, just crush it flat. They should pause and reflect a lot more.

In the most extreme form, this represents an inverted form of Marxism. They want people and communities to get out of the way of history. Remove all restraints on the market, or else! Stop complaining about the car industry shutting down and your once beautiful suburb descending into welfare-supported decay, they say, because by ripping away support for these things, we're creating a wealthier future. Your poverty is your children's wealth (or, at least, the wealth of somebody else's children in some richer suburb closer to the city). It might be pointed out that Stalin offered the Ukrainian peasantry much the same deal: stop standing in the way of the new economic revolution; stop holding up the future; get with the program. Here we have the philosophical essence of creative destruction: a historical and moral vacuum which heartless ideologues can fill with their crazy schemes to remake the world. And it turns out to be a historical ploy that is as false as it is shallow. Its origins are worth examining.

We're awash these days with the Big Picture. Narrative – that's the key to good communications, isn't it! Once upon a time, these narratives were formulated by historians. Years ago, for example, when asked what they intended to read on their summer holidays, our political leaders would almost invariably say, 'The latest volume of Manning Clark's *History of Australia*.' Whether, once they got to the beach, they actually read Manning Clark or the racing form guide was immaterial; the point was that they needed to give us a sense that they understood the river of history and where its mighty course was taking us. Nowadays, they're more likely to tell you they're reading the latest brace of books about the Great Australian Economic Miracle by senior newspaper columnists. This is because, today, our nation's grand narrative is told almost exclusively by economic journalists. The odd serious-minded economist who once helped lead policy from within the PM's office has a go, but usually fails to reach the bestseller lists, even in the high-brow indie bookshops. Such works tend to tell the same story: How We Made the Transition to a Modern Market Economy and Became the Envy of the World (and How We Will Continue to Make It as Long as We Forget All that Nonsense about Equality).

The thing we are transitioning from tends to be represented in the same way. Economically, it was corporatist, protected, insular, overregulated, heavily unionised, militant, seemingly always on strike and therefore criminally unproductive. Culturally, it was embarrassingly unsophisticated in the way all life seemingly was before the espresso machine: the men had large sideburns and wore wide-lapelled suits, big-collared shirts and fat ties; the women had beehive hair-dos and skimpy bikinis and drooled at surfing hunks; everyone drank generic-tasting tap beer and instant coffee, drove Toranas, Geminis and (of course) Leyland P-76s, and endlessly sought the approval of boorish, bored celebrities visiting from overseas. All up, these books tell us, the old times were misogynist, racist, lazy and – and here's the real message – complacent, complacency being the most wicked of our modern sins.

It's interesting to watch the former politicians, economists and public policymakers who gave us The Transition talking about the past in the numerous documentaries made on the subject. When they reach the 1970s they tend to slip into comedy; with broad smiles breaking out on their faces, they say things like: 'Just as they thought it was acceptable to listen to glam rock (ha, ha), they thought governments should control foreign investment,' or 'They thought they could determine the exchange rate of the dollar,' or 'They seriously reckoned they had the right to go on strike.' 'Can you believe it?' their sneers imply, as the camera holds them in focus for a few seconds longer. You see, when it comes down to it, to the creative destroyers the past was simply corrupt, one great self-indulgent orgy like a Sodom and Gomorrah scene in a Cecil B. DeMille movie, something that must be expunged, vaporised, paved over, replaced.

To replace this Old Testament narrative, they've given us a new one, which always seems to begin with the same words: 'And then there was Paul ..' Paul and his disciples led the way into the new future, where we dropped all that nonsense about full employment and collective bargaining, cut corporate and high marginal taxes, discovered China and the rest of Asia, created a pool of capital through compulsory superannuation and laid the foundation for three decades of economic growth that even the biggest global recession since the Great Depression couldn't stop, et cetera, et cetera, ad infinitum. St Paul and his followers did it, St John and his crew didn't oppose it, and we all saw that it was good; so sayeth the Lord.

The sheer predictability of these narratives gives the game away. (I dare you to open the *Australian* or the *Australian Financial Review* tomorrow morning and not find an echo of them.) They comprise a hero narrative, obviously: with time fast running out (time is always running out where economic reform is concerned), a handful of heroic men and women, firm in their convictions, set out to save the nation from itself, and succeeded just before the International Monetary Fund had to step in. The narrative is not so much an economic analysis as a moral judgment handed down from the mountaintop (or, rather, the boardroom on the fiftieth floor), ordering adherence to a set of new commandments: thou shalt not restrain competition; thou shalt not go against free trade; thou shalt not deny the shareholders; thou shalt not deform the labour market by forming a union; thou shalt not redistribute wealth; and so on. You can find similar narratives in Britain and America; only the names change.

Something similar was happening in George Orwell's time. He was at once fascinated and horrified by the Marxist obsession with reinterpreting and rewriting history, especially economic history. He recognised that those seeking to overthrow the way we live tend to start by falsifying the past – because it is only by discrediting the good things about the past that such people can make the present seem better and the utopian future they are offering seem inevitable, when in fact life in many ways has become worse. This is the meaning of the famous party slogan from Orwell's dark novel *Nineteen Eighty-Four*: 'Who controls the past controls the future: who controls the present controls the past.' By misrepresenting and discrediting the time before the Great Australian Economic Miracle, by portraying it as complacent and corrupt and laughable and poor, our present narrators are clearing away the positive human memories that might restrain their attempts to create a future that is 100 per cent safe for productivity.

In a famous scene from the novel, the character Winston Smith goes into a proletarian pub to talk to someone old enough to remember what life was like before the revolution, but finds that, under the onslaught of propaganda and mindless popular culture, the old man's memory has turned to rubble. How long will it be, we might ask, before there is anyone who still remembers that the past was in many respects superior to the present, and who knows that the future can in fact be different from the one now being foisted upon us?

The economists' hero narrative runs into an immediate problem. It is forced to recognise that the greasy-haired, wide-lapelled, Holden-driving past was in many ways a success on its own terms – and popular. Just view the images on the TV documentaries: crowds of people surging into factory gates; newspaper headlines screaming 'full employment achieved'; highways full of Australian-made cars that people loved to drive; Australians at play on the beach, eating steak around the barbecue in the backyards of houses that were affordable to working people, safe from worry because their children's education was free, Medibank was free, their regulated weekends were free; a political system that, by the middle of the 1970s, was modernising, optimistic, at once liberal and social-democratic, reforming and conserving. The truth is that the generations that were in charge of our nation prior to the 1980s created a society that was in many ways more successful and popular than the one the economic reformers have given us. It gave Australians a standard of living and a way of life which was the envy of the world – but which the economists, especially the creative destroyers, can only view as complacent. The economic growth of the past came with full employment. The creative destroyers' growth has not. Whose is superior?

Third, language and the meaning of words. As well as reclaiming the past, we have to reclaim language, especially the meaning of the word 'reform'. By giving themselves the title of 'reformers', the people who brought us the Great Australian Economic Miracle imbue themselves with a moral authority and a democratic mandate that they don't really possess. Who could reasonably be against reform – the removal of faults or errors to promote change for the better? No one. But in the arena of political economy, 'reform' has a meaning far deeper and richer than the one the self-styled economic reformers are offering us.

In its original political and economic usage, 'reform' was a nineteenth-century movement that set out to build a sounder moral basis for the new economy being created so rapidly by the Industrial Revolution, the faults of which were highlighted (either directly or by implication) by the great thinkers and writers of the day, most notably Charles Dickens, William Blake, Elizabeth Gaskell, Charlotte Bronte and many others no longer commonly read today. The Reform Acts to democratise the House of Commons were joined by Factory Acts, Mines Acts and other pieces of social legislation that limited the length of the working day, prevented the economic exploitation of children, gave people the right to join trade unionists, and improved public education and public health through, among other things, improved sanitation. (The eight-hour day movement here in Australia was part of this great reform era.) Reformers did more than remove outdated controls on the market; they also stopped the gerrymandering of parliament, ended the slave trade, prevented children as young as five years old from going down mines, and created the moral basis for the great improvements in life that were continued by social democracy into the twentieth century.

To place the freeing of the dollar, the introduction of the GST and the attempt to replace collective bargaining with individual contracts on the same moral plane as the great reforms of the past 200 years is a faux hero narrative indeed, absurd and delusional in equal parts, the sort of egotistical tribute that vice pays to virtue. The true reforming efforts of the nineteenth century were motivated in large part by moral concerns, whereas the faux reforming efforts of our time are usually motivated by a desire to remove moral concerns from economic policy almost completely, taking us back to the era of Gradgrind and his world, in which the reason of the market was completely unrestrained.

Fourth, sociology. Here's another fact we need to grasp if we want to create a better future: the Australian working class is not the reactionary mass that many – including many on the Left – sometimes take it to be. These days, in certain circles, when the subject of working-class Australia comes up, the response is often negative. Recently, at a dinner for the visiting English intellectual Maurice Glasman, I heard the following response from someone at my table: 'I agree with everything he said about the economy, except of course for all that praise of the working class and its values.' These days, when educated people of the Right and Left think about the old Anglo-Saxon and European working class, they conjure up a mass of negative adjectives: xenophobia is usually the first, followed perhaps by sexism and homophobia, then anti-intellectualism, and finally (usually without irony) avarice. This view leads to policies of the worst sort as the political parties attempt to appeal to these negative stereotypes: the demonising of refugees, opposition to same-sex marriage, the creation of dumbed-down subjects at poorer public schools, the rubbishing of universities and the life of the mind, and a simplistic, populist approach to holding down the rising cost of living (which no one ever actually manages to do, despite all the hand-on-heart promises they make). It ends up with all parties, including Labor, pursuing a sterile, transactional form of politics that offers a combination of financial bribes and punitive social policy instead of a vision of a better society. It's a formula that never delivers Labor victory, and simply robs it of its sense of purpose.

Such nonsense about working-class attitudes is easily debunked; all it requires is a few conversations. On one of my visits to the Holden plant at Dandenong, I got talking to one of the now retired chief engineers. He'd come to Australia from India in March 1974 and had got a job at the plant virtually the next day, working on the truck assembly line. He freely admits it was another world in which you sometimes needed a thick skin to survive. The foreman, for example, had names for everyone in his section of the line, most of which consisted of four letters. (This foreman was obviously not my father, who never swore and would cuff me if I ever did.) On hearing this, I asked the man whether he ever experienced racism while working at Holden. 'No,' he said. 'Never.' In fact, with the help of Holden he went on to become one of the plant's leading engineering managers, and he later used this experience to take a sabbatical of sorts, when he worked for one of the world's premier motor-racing teams. Working-class racism obviously never held him back.

One of the managers of the current spare parts operation also told me that racism had never been an issue at the plant; in fact, he said, the only ethnic tension he had ever had to deal with since he started at the plant back in 1979 involved tensions between workers from different sides of the civil war in the former Yugoslavia in the early 1990s, and even then it was mild stuff.

Why is this important? Why does it matter so much that Australians, but especially Labor and the Left, should drop the misconception that the working class are beyond the pale in their beliefs? Because without the working class, social democracy loses most of its purpose. When you think about it, social democracy was founded on the very idea that the people with the least wealth, privilege and power can and should be a force for social change – because they have a direct and obvious interest in creating a more equal society. Once you regard the working class as reactionary, vulgar and stupid – even vaguely sinister and to be feared, as my friend at the Glasman lecture implied – the game is up. But this has been mostly forgotten.

As the educated middle class has grown, many on the Left have come to see it – supposedly more rational and amenable to progressive causes – as their new agent of change. But no matter what their progressive beliefs, the middle class, especially many highly educated middle-class people who form a progressive elite, will never be a sufficient force for greater economic and social equality, and can never be fully relied upon to worry about the fate of places like Doveton. This is not because they are intrinsically uncaring people, but because when it comes down to it, they benefit from such inequality and tend to be ignorant about its true nature and extent, no matter how hard they try to understand. Unless we truly care about the working class and the communities in which its members live, and unless we take their economic and social interests seriously, there will be no advances in economic and social equality. This is why the Labor Party and the Left cannot afford to cut itself off from the union movement, and it is why both must clean up their internal affairs and get their acts together as a matter of extreme seriousness and urgency.

Fifth, aesthetics, particularly creativity. Another important way of thinking about what's going on concerns aesthetics, particularly urban aesthetics and the creation of beautiful objects. This is an area of crucial importance, although it isn't often in the forefront of our minds – until, that is, we see it with our own eyes. Urban beauty is typically something we associate with the wealthy and highly educated. We expect their inner-suburban streets to be neat and leafy, their apartments to be old and art-deco or new and sharp-edged, and their holiday homes to look like spaceships that have parked themselves on ocean cliff-tops. We value this sort of beauty and prefer it to ugly squalor every time – and we do so for innate reasons that can't be quantified on a spreadsheet. We tend to put this down to the superior taste of the people who live in such desirable places, but in reality it's down to their superior bank balances. They may have a monopoly on expensive real estate and A-list architects, but can they possibly have a monopoly on finer human feelings? Show a working person a gracious mansion or an art-filled penthouse and he or she will choose it over a crumbling former public housing estate every time.

The fact that older working-class suburbs don't look as nice as they once did, and sometimes look downright ugly, is something that should concern us because it affects everyone. Drive through the neighbourhoods with the highest rates of unemployment and you will likely see an unattractiveness that is unnecessary and self-perpetuating: broken or missing fences, rusting cars and unkempt lawns, and in the worst places shuttered shops, smashed windows, graffiti-scarred walls and burnt-out buildings. To put it simply, nobody wants it.

Although it was purpose-built for the families of factory workers, when my neighbourhood in Doveton was first constructed it was well planned and attractively laid out. Serious consideration was given to the look and feel of the streets, with plenty of parks with colourful children's play equipment, public gardens opposite strip shopping centres, with even the trees and hedges in front yards well-chosen by the Housing Commission that built and then helped maintain it all. The planners of these places were in touch with the mass of the people in a way that public-policy experts tend not to be today. Aside from the obvious economic consequences of letting these sorts of neighbourhoods go – falling property values compounding year on year, aspirational flight, the concentration of people living on welfare, rising crime and so forth, all producing a downward spiral that is expensive to arrest – it naturally makes people feel depressed. Imagine waking up each morning, opening your blinds and seeing a sea of rusting trucks or a vacant block with weeds six feet high, littered with discarded bedding, whitegoods and syringes, a haven for bored teenagers to vandalise or take drugs. This, now, is a reality for many people.

If a concern with beauty seems an elite obsession, and one unrelated to a social-democratic agenda, think again. In purely utilitarian terms, beautifying our working-class suburbs would bring greater benefit and pleasure to more people's lives than any number of highbrow art galleries, which of course are so generously endowed by the super-rich. Why can't we have both? Indeed, one might plausibly say that a revulsion against urban ugliness was one of the original and most important motivating elements of social-democratic politics. After all, calling a workplace a 'dark satanic mill' is an aesthetic as well as a moral judgment. Here is Friedrich Engels – a founder of modern social democracy – describing the industrial suburbs of Manchester in the 1840s:

The cottages are old, dirty and of the smallest sort, the streets uneven, fallen into ruts and in part without drains or pavement; masses of refuse, offal and sickening filth lie among standing pools in all directions ... The race that lives in these ruinous cottages, behind broken windows, mended with oilskin, sprung doors, and rotten door-posts, or in dark, wet cellars, in measureless filth and stench, in this atmosphere penned in as with a purpose, this race must really have reached the lowest stage of humanity.

This idea that the lives of everyday people could be improved by beautifying their surroundings is at the heart of the work of one of the greatest nineteenth-century socialist thinkers, William Morris, who, in addition to being a political activist, was an artist, poet and close friend of Pre-Raphaelite painter Dante Gabriel Rossetti and the poet Robert Browning. Morris grasped something that has relevance today and which puts the graph-wielding managerialists in their place: that progress can be measured by more than money. People don't want to live in the most expensive neighbourhood they can afford, but the most beautiful one, and they want jobs that are not only well paid but also satisfying. Early social democracy was all about such things, not just more money, but we have forgotten this.

How can we have forgotten about the importance of the quality of the work we do and the satisfaction it brings to our lives? There's a certain nobility in making things, especially things of obvious utility or beauty, and this makes craftsmanship something we should strive to preserve. Think of our workers at Holden in Dandenong; they didn't just collect widgets as they dropped from a conveyor belt, they made highly complex and beautiful machines that required skill and effort, and this gave them an enormous sense of satisfaction – certainly greater than that gained by staring at a computer screen all day or manning a consumer help desk. If we don't value this sort of thing, what do we value?

It's true that, even in the strongest manufacturing economy, not everyone can build cars and submarines and components for airliners; for some, catching a widget or responding to a disgruntled consumer has to be enough. But we rob our society and ourselves of something important when we fail to recognise the broad value of industrial craftsmanship and the opportunity it provides for the millions of people who happen not to be 'artists' to have such obviously meaningful occupations. Giving people the chance to lead creative lives should be an important objective of public policy.

Recently, the National Gallery of Victoria made exactly this point when it staged a major artistic exhibition of Australian-manufactured cars. It even featured the Valiant Charger muscle car owned by my next-door neighbour; how beautiful it was. Walking around the exhibition brought home to me the fact that every time we farm such

meaningful work out to other countries (who unasham-
edly or underhandedly practise the sort of industry protection we find morally beneath us), a part of our quality
of life gets exported along with it. These are the sorts of
things that, in their unconsciously philistine way, the economic reformers neither measure nor value, and which
they might unthinkingly dismiss as 'rent-seeking', but
which ordinary people who haven't been to university
understand intuitively to be an important part of life. By
creating a spreadsheet that closes a factory, even the most
artistically inclined economic reformer can unconsciously
condemn thousands of creative everyday people to lives of
pointless boredom. Creativity should be better understood and valued more.

Morality, history, linguistic precision, sociology, aesthetics: adding these to our thinking would allow us to
honour the complexity, generosity, creativity and even
majesty of working-class life and work in wider and more
honest ways than economics alone makes possible. Yes,
economics has something to say, but on its own it tells us
almost nothing.

Ordinary people do not live their lives according to
the sort of narrow parameters that can be plotted on
graphs. Their thinking on economic, social and political
issues doesn't revolve around the concept of productivity
but around whether their children have jobs to look forward to, whether they can afford to buy a home, their
level of employment security, the quality of their jobs, the

physical state of their neighbourhoods, and the civility or otherwise they encounter in their daily lives – and all these things at once.

Politicians nowadays try automatically to reduce these concrete concerns to supposedly measurable concepts such as 'cost of living', and they roll everyone together under the nonsensical imported American term 'working families'. Why is this? Is it cynicism? Is it because they haven't the capacity to stand up to the pollsters who bribe them with promises of easy victory, or the tabloid editors and shock jocks who bully them with simplistic and anti-intellectual explanations of what ordinary people really care about? Or is it because politicians and their advisers today lack the wider education, the imagination or the verbal capacity necessary to articulate something broader, deeper and more meaningful, something that can move people in genuine and even profound ways?

The management consultants and the pollsters don't have the answers, and it's time we tell them: 'Enough!'

We need to connect, now more than ever. This is becoming increasingly urgent. Some would say it is *the* urgent issue of the day. But how are we to do it?

It is a common complaint of the creative destroyers that our political system is broken – broken because economic reform is no longer possible. At election after election, governments that advocate privatisation and cut thousands of public-sector jobs are being tossed out or having their majorities slashed. The economic reformers and their boosters in the press tell us that we, the people, led by populists the way a beef farmer leads a bull by its nose ring, are the problem, and that we must be ignored for the good of the country. What politicians must do, they say, is prepare the electorate for uncomfortable truths by providing them with a new narrative, and ideally one which involves multiplying the current rate of productivity by two or three. The debate about this narrative and the policies that flow from it, they argue, must be taken out of the public arena and discussed in forums insulated from the special pleading of vested interests and the emotion of the electorate.

For some, this means a new economic forum of wise economists, led by the old advisers from the glory days of the 1980s and '90s. For others, it means a national summit of businessmen and sensible welfare leaders, led by the productivity commissioners and the men who brought us the Great Australian Economic Miracle: Hawke, Keating, Howard, Costello and their former advisers. With the exceptions of the prime minister, the treasurer and a few other office-holders who can be relied upon to support the Productivity Commission's line, all current members of parliament must be excluded. Only in this way – by locking out the people and their democratically elected representatives, and thus by engineering an appointed Parliament of Creative Destruction – can economic reform be certain of coming out on top.

In other words, democracy can't be trusted to get things done, and economics must be made safe from it, safe from the potential losers from change, safe from the human yearning for equality and creativity, safe from moral reasoning, safe from the memory of something better. This is essentially the same lament about people power first mouthed by the elites in fifth-century Athens, but whereas the Athenians said, 'Leave the decisions to the philosopher kings,' we say, 'Leave them to the economists.' Like the Eastern European communists before them, the creative destroyers have finally found the root of their problem: to succeed in their plans, they first need to elect a new people.

They know that, out in the open, their philosophy of creative destruction is doomed because the people are wary of it. You can't smash what's left of the car industry, put the remaining canneries out of production and replace their produce with contaminated food from China, get rid of penalty rates and the minimum wage, privatise what's left of electricity and rail and ports, make people pay to visit bulk-billing doctors when their children are sick, price university degrees at $100,000, break what remains of union power, shift an even greater share of GDP from labour to capital, make more people redundant at the age of fifty, murder more neighbourhoods and destroy more lives without expecting a democratic fight. The Australian people do not want these things, and never will.

This has enormous significance for our democracy. If our political system is really broken, as the common slogan today says, it is because while the reformers want creative destruction, the people do not. The popular will is being subverted. The people may be willing to accept change, but they are unwilling to accept change for change's sake, or for the sole sake of the people at the top. Bringing these two sides of our democracy back together requires our politicians to listen to the people.

It comes down to this: change can't be avoided. Everyone knows that. But just because change can't be avoided, it doesn't mean that everything has to change at once, or that it has to change in the way decreed from on high. This is not an argument for replacing hard reckoning about the present with some naive form of nostalgia. We can't create a time machine and we shouldn't try. But perhaps nostalgia can sometimes have a point, because when we look back we can attempt to understand what the past got right, and we can see that sometimes our parents' generation got it more right than we have. The idea that life in the future will always be better than it is now is just as naive as the idea that the past was always better.

There is an alternative. There are many imaginable futures, and it seems to me that the future the people *will* accept is the one that adequately respects important elements of the past, not one that tries to wipe the past out and simply start again. This requires an effort: we must think for ourselves as a people, and not accept the tired, imported, out-of-date, out-of-time, off-the-shelf theory of creative destruction that is being offered as our only option.

We need instead to choose a future that – like the past – is designed to benefit all the Australian people, not just some. It's the future we were heading towards before the unfortunate revolutionary changes of the past thirty years derailed it. Back before that time – an era still within the span of middle-aged memory – we believed our economic future lay in making things, and we believed our social future lay in supporting communities. We saw ourselves as more than just an agglomeration of individual consumers left to fend for themselves. For the people of Doveton, this meant making cars, trucks, trains and processed food, and it meant supporting neighbourhoods that were built around job creation and the provision of real opportunities for ordinary people. It meant nation-building for every member of the nation.

Thanks to sometimes unstoppable change, but also to stupid, shortsighted and overly theoretical policy – the too hasty closing down of car manufacturing in the face of a temporarily overvalued dollar being but the worst example – we can't any longer make all the sorts of things we once did. But we can aspire to make things, to create skilled jobs, to value creativity, to replace urban blight with urban regeneration, not in the bits-and-pieces way we currently do, as a sort of penance for smashing things up in the first place, but with real purpose and real investment. The way our parents lived, and the sort of egalitarian nation they worked and fought for, provides us not so much with a model but with the moral inspiration we need to get started.

Go out and look for it, because it is still there. *Sous les pavés, la plage!*

CONCLUSION
TO REALLY CARE

The impulse of the senses ... and the conclusions of Reason,
draw men together; but the Imagination is the true fire
stolen from heaven ...

—MARY WOLLSTONECRAFT

I thought I'd finished my modest little story about Doveton, but I decided to spend another week or so searching for some positive things to say – some green shoots, a little hope; God knows the place needs it.

I'll admit my motivations for doing so weren't totally honourable. When you write honestly about somewhere going through hard times, you inevitably encounter criticisms of the 'How dare he?' type. 'He's a blow-in ... he's talking the place down when what it needs is talking up ... he's not here battling away every day like us ... he's overlooked all the positive economic development that's going on ... why didn't he talk to me?' and so on. All of that, obviously, contains an element of truth, even if you ignore the fact that I've cared enough about my old home town to spend half a year writing a book about it. Anyway, it's just as big a mistake sometimes to artificially talk a place up. There are affluent people in Doveton, certainly, but writing about Doveton to illustrate affluence is about as enlightening as writing about Toorak to illustrate the adverse effects of unemployment – it might exist, but it's hardly typical.

I spend a day in meetings with economic development experts in the City of Casey and the City of Greater Dandenong. (Doveton, which lies on their boundary, is technically in the former but historically linked to the latter.) I'm impressed by the economic development efforts being made and come away with a folder two inches thick, full of glossy strategies, plans, partnerships, regeneration initiatives, stakeholder newsletters and the usual offspring of the marriage between management consultants and highly committed municipal officials.

And it does indeed seem that there is much going on, some of which I can see from the cafe at which one of the meetings takes place. The cafe is part of a Revitalising Central Dandenong initiative, which opens up the city centre and links it to the railway station and a new shopping plaza – the locals refer to the new development as the Pompidou Centre. Panda – who, as the former state member for the area, was involved in the planning – had taken me on a tour of it a couple of months before, and locals rightly regard it as a symbol of how things can be improved if you try hard enough. The problem is that from my seat in the café, looking out into Dandenong's main street, it's all too obvious why this new development and a lot more like it are needed.

At the end of the meeting I take a walk down the street, and in two blocks count forty-three shopfronts, of which four are untenanted, four are $2 shops, one is a pokies venue, one is a charity shop, and three are variations on the 'buy, sell and cash loan' businesses that in generations past would have been called pawnbrokers. I walk into one of them and see the usual collection of household items offloaded by people desperate for cash, some of whom, perhaps having already disposed of the kids' Xbox for $100, are standing at the counter and negotiating desperately needed loans which, in the long run, will likely make their finances worse.

This brings back a bad memory of a single desperate moment my father had when he and I were alone together in Doveton, and it strikes me that the owners of these businesses are attracted to poverty like sharks to a school of pilchards. Don't you hate them? I also find the Coles Variety Store outlet where my Aunt Ena sold the garments her mother made; it is now one of those discount chemist chains filled with disorienting fluorescent lights.

A few days before my meeting in the new Pompidou Centre, local manufacturers used its forecourt to put on a display called 'Dandenong on Wheels'. Featuring sophisticated trucks, trams, buses, emergency vehicles, garbage trucks and campervans, the exhibition showed off some of the high-tech manufacturing going on in the area. It was reported prominently in the *Age* the next day, but the *AFR* went instead with a feature story on an amazing high-tech Siemens factory in Amberg, in south-east Germany (where, coincidentally, Aunt Ena was interned in a Displaced Persons' camp at the end of World War II), and another about how deregulating the car import market further will slash the price of a Ferrari from $525,000 to just $343,000. Now that they've stopped people like my father building cars, they're planning to stop them selling them too. It's clear that creating jobs for the little people in Doveton is of zero interest to the readers of financial newspapers, even though their investment decisions might make a positive difference.

It's obvious that manufacturing is gradually regaining a toehold here. Could it be the hope the people of Doveton are looking for? Later, after talking to the organiser of the local manufacturing alliance, I decide to take a tour of the great manufacturing conurbation that is opening up to the south of Dandenong, stretching all the way to Mentone and Frankston. Driving along with massive trucks tailgating me all the way, I explore huge industrial parks (there are six on the map I am given), where concrete buildings are going up to house a mixture of medium-sized and boutique modern 'factories'. This is going to grow – that's obvious. The caravan manufacturer Jayco, for instance, where Fred worked for a while after leaving Heinz, recently put on another 200 workers, taking its workforce to 1000, and is even doing its best to give jobs to locals with drug, alcohol and other problems; more power to them, I say. It's not on the scale of the old days, when GMH alone had between 4500 and 5000 workers on its payroll, but it's impressive nonetheless.

Still, I can't help but point out to the economic development officials that while manufacturing appears to be returning, unemployment in Doveton, very literally just over the road from some of these factories, is still significantly over 20 per cent. How can that be? They tell me, as a sort of afterthought: the sad reality is that despite the efforts of companies like Jayco, the new manufacturing jobs being created in the area are unlikely be filled by many people from Doveton. The clean, sleek futuristic factories (like the Siemens factory in Amberg), with their high-tech processes, need employees with medium to high-level trade qualifications, and even university degrees, but poor old Doveton has one of the least educated and least qualified populations in the state. And because it has become a destination for the least-educated refugees and asylum seekers from the poorest communities of Africa, Asia and the Middle East, much of Doveton's workforce can't even speak enough English to read a health and safety sign, never mind operate complex computer-based equipment. Many, because of their asylum seeker status, are not even legally permitted to work.

I decide to attend the National Manufacturing Week exhibition in Melbourne, where I'm told employers from the Dandenong region will be present in large numbers.

It's obvious the moment I walk in that manufacturing in the future is going to be lean – perhaps too lean for places like Doveton to benefit.

What stands out most are the robots. There are dozens on display, some of which look like programmable lathes and saws, but others which look like one-armed factory workers. I decide to make a pain of myself by asking difficult questions about the economic and employment effects of these human-like devices. It turns out that robots will save manufacturers serious money by reducing their wages bills. The salespeople give me calculations based on differing wage rates and on-costs.

For example, at a 3 per cent interest rate, a $25,000 robot that works twenty-four hours a day, seven days a week (including Christmas Day and Good Friday), costs just twenty cents per hour, plus electricity. My sister's friend Cheryl costs $16.86. But when I press the point of what this is going to mean for unskilled workers, I'm told that it will have no effect on unemployment. 'You see, the business owners who introduce robot workers aren't doing it for financial reasons, but to relieve their valued employees of boring, repetitive tasks.' They're philanthropists, philosophers even, doing their employees a favour.

But after fifteen minutes of pressing for an answer, I'm told about a model factory in Belgium where 150 robots are supervised by just six humans, making it incredibly profitable. And anyway, you can't get good human help anymore, even when there is high unemployment – the lazy proles just don't want to work. This claim is illustrated by anecdote after anecdote about languid factory hands who don't pay attention to their tasks.

At one display I spot three of the $25,000 robots performing simple, repetitive tasks next to each other in a sort of mock assembly line. I ask the engineer if they could be put to use on a food canning and packing line, say, at Heinz. 'Oh, yes,' he says. 'That one could put on the lids, that one could put on the labels, and that bigger one could lift the cans into boxes, then cart them off to a truck on a computer-controlled conveyor belt.' I tell him I'm naming them Audrey, Dawn and Pamela, after my mother and two sisters whose jobs they would have taken, had they been around a few decades before. He isn't impressed.

My line of questioning is a little unfair, I admit, as the robot salespeople aren't philosophers, just decent businesspeople trying to keep their own companies (located in China, Japan and Switzerland) alive, but I find this inability to engage in serious discussion of the social consequences of their technology a little annoying. One day we're all going to pay for this unwillingness to think through what eliminating millions of low-skilled jobs will do to our society. Places like Doveton already know. When the computers eventually come for middle-class jobs – a process already underway – every suburb is going to get a taste of what it feels like to live in my old home town.

I guess it comes down to the fact that the old factory world provided an organising principle for a society that worked, if not perfectly, at least reasonably well. It provided jobs, skills, a sense of purpose, generalised affluence and even a democratic political logic – with parties for labour and parties for business that, over time, balanced each other out to a tolerable degree. Looked at this way, there's something inherently democratic, even social-democratic, about an economy based on mass-employment manufacturing, because in an economy in which their labour is in demand, the little people are in charge – or at least not easy to ignore. This is what democracy is supposed to be about: people power. But what sort of society is a robotic economy going to produce? One with even more places like Doveton. And perhaps one without a viable social-democratic Labor Party – a process that may already have begun.

If the next generation from Doveton is to get a toehold in this new economy, where are its members to get the necessary skills from? To find out, I visit a refuge of otherwise abandoned optimism: Doveton College. It sits on top of the highest hill in the suburb, next to the swimming pool at which Panda, Jimmy and I learned to swim, and on a sunny day in autumn it feels like a sunbeam of hope is shining down upon it. The principal, Greg McMahon, has been sent in to rescue the place after a not totally satisfactory beginning when the college opened in 2012. A good citizen, the wealthy health-industry entrepreneur Julius Colman, pumped serious money from his foundation into a joint plan with the Labor state government of John Brumby to regenerate schooling in the suburb by amalgamating four existing schools – the ones now being smashed up by vandals – into a 'birth to Year 9 community learning centre'. It's very literally that: bringing together babies in childcare, toddlers in play-based long daycare, and Prep to Year 9 school students in a comprehensive project to combat the effects of social disadvantage.

In fact, the school goes much further than Prep to Year 9, because to succeed in helping these children, it has to educate their often unemployed and semi-literate parents as well. About 20 per cent of the pupils, McMahon estimates, come from troubled families afflicted by long-term unemployment, domestic violence, mental-health problems and trauma related to torture or civil war. While I'm there, a police unit arrives with some unpleasant duty to perform. The school also has to take on some basic tasks such as feeding the children, many of whom get more than three-quarters of their daily nutrition while at school. Asylum seeker children, who aren't legally entitled to attend the school, also have to be sought out and helped in a sort of extracurricular duty. No one else is going to do it. These people, I conclude, are saints.

Principal McMahon is extremely generous with his time, and after a chat takes me around to meet some students and teachers at lunchtime. He seems to know just about all of them by name, and we have purposeful conversations with kids of all ethnic backgrounds, who are mixing and playing well together in the playground. We meet one little girl, about five or six years old and bright as a button, who happily tells us that she has just got a new book from the school library; she shows it to us proudly. We stop and help her phonetically spell out the title, *Jam for Nana*.

We also visit the childcare centre, where some children are having their afternoon nap, and another one runs up to hug us and say hello. We meet mothers having lunch who are doing Certificate III courses in Education Support, with the objective of becoming classroom assistants. Having the parents attend like this, McMahon tells me, is a good way to ensure their children also come to school each day; here, that is not a given. He also tells me that while the Gonski school funding model was designed for places like this, and the school would have got more money than any other, Doveton College hasn't seen a cent. All those promises the managerialists made, and not a cent.

You can't come away from a place like this without having at least some part of your heart warmed. These people are doing the toughest job there is; they, not the overpaid principals of the better private schools, are the unsung heroes of our education system, and they need more help. But I have misgivings about the place, and they stem from something not of the principal's doing and not in his control: the school has been asked to make up for the total collapse of the local economy and the society it supported.

Here are the human results of three decades of economic devastation and humanitarian settlement – babies, toddlers, children, adolescents and their second-generation-unemployed parents – concentrated into a single place that's meant to be a crèche, kindergarten, primary school, secondary school, welfare agency, even canteen. It mixes together the old poor with the newly arrived poor, the long-term unemployed with those unable to speak English. Why is it, I ask myself, that poor people always have to do all the heavy lifting for other poor people? The wealthy think they do it through progressive taxation, endlessly calling for more tax relief, but they're kidding themselves, as usual.

I want to be wrong, but it seems a hope against hope that Doveton College will be able to make up entirely for the one thing that is more likely than anything else to account for Doveton's problems: the total lack of jobs suitable for the students' parents. Maybe it will work, maybe it won't, although it's worth a try – but when Panda and Jimmy and I and our other friends were children in Doveton, we didn't need schools that were designed as welfare agencies because our mothers and our fathers and our older brothers and sisters all had jobs. Give the parents jobs and the school might work as a springboard to success, as the old Doveton High School which my friends and I attended did. Try as they might, schools on their own cannot make up for the failure of the economy to deliver affluence for everyone, and it's hard to believe that serious policymakers haven't thought about this and done something more besides. But they simply haven't. It's about class, not classrooms.

On my way home, I stop to get a Coke at the old milk bar, now $2 shop, near where I lived. I notice that the front windows have been smashed but not fully replaced, and are being held together by some temporary transparent film. This is the second smashed window I've seen at this strip shopping centre since my study began. I ask the young man who serves me, who looks to be about eighteen, what happened. His father caught some juvenile shoplifters, who, resentful at being so accused, returned after midnight to throw bricks through the window in revenge. Perhaps they got the bricks from the wreck of my old local primary school, just around the corner.

He's a nice kid, and when I tell him this was where my mother worked forty years ago, he tells me that his family bought the shop the year before and are doing it up to make it into a cafe. The walls have recently been resurfaced and painted, and I can suddenly see that things just might improve – after the windows are replaced, that is. It's another ray of hope, if a small one. A good cafe might just make the place a little busier and more pleasant, and perhaps encourage a few people with jobs to buy into the area. Who knows? I resolve to return later in the year for a coffee and some of his mother's homemade Serbian cake.

During my journey home, I'm caught in a traffic jam next to Melbourne Grammar School at pick-up time. In front of me, a mother in a black Porsche SUV searches for a parking spot. (A *Porsche* SUV? I can't figure out what angers me more – the fact that Porsche makes such ridiculous cars, the fact that someone feels the need to choose such a vulgar status symbol, or the fact that Australia's car factories had to close to make this degree of automobile choice possible.) Through a sea of Audis and BMWs, I can see students in expensive-looking blue sports uniforms playing soccer on the lush sports grounds next to the Shrine of Remembrance, the late-afternoon sun glowing. It strikes me that these schools – with their sense of entitlement and all their talk of moral leadership and *noblesse oblige*, which get so much but give so little, and which actually got their Gonski funding guarantees while poor old Doveton College got none – should be the ones who have to take on the educational disadvantage of Doveton. Why not make schools like this take a busload of kids from places like Doveton in return for all the funding they get?

If that sounds mad, it's only because society has lost its capacity for moral reasoning. If only, I muse, I could be education minister for a day ...

Thoughts like that bring me to a conclusion of sorts. During my journeys back to Doveton, something has gradually become apparent to me, and it hits me between the eyes on my last days there. When it comes down to it, few outsiders care about Doveton – and I mean *really* care, in the way necessary to actually change things. I think some of my friends in the Labor Party care, but sometimes perhaps not as much as they care about productivity. If they really cared, things wouldn't have been allowed to get so dire.

At the Dandenong Magistrates' Court, where I sat in for part of a morning, hearing case after case in which the real problems were unemployment and family break-down and heroin and ice, a magistrate tells me that, almost without fail, even the saddest cases – and there are 20,000 a year at this court alone – agree that what they really need to turn their lives around is a job, a home and someone to love. A job, a home and someone to love – it seems pretty basic, doesn't it? But for all our supposed policy sophistication, for all the claims that we're better than our parents' generation at running our country, we don't get this. We can't conceptualise social problems in human ways anymore, and we have only managed to turn parts of our society into a pipeline from school to gaol. It's one of the prices you pay for the single-minded pursuit of productivity.

Our policymakers have no answer to all this. From talking to them, one gets the distinct impression that even the local leaders would rather that Doveton, which sits as a grim postage stamp of dysfunction on the maps of their otherwise expanding and booming municipalities, is a hopeless case, best kept hidden lest it draw too much attention away from all the good news stories that can be told (of which there are many). They've reconceived Doveton in their minds, changing it from a destination in which people live to a place people travel through to get to somewhere better. The place has become a highway for as yet unmet aspirations rather than a community in which true happiness for the majority can flourish. You see, Doveton doesn't matter as a policy problem, because its community doesn't exist as a reality – much like Heraclitus's famous stream into which you can never step twice. By such feats of economic reforming logic we seem to have concluded that Doveton and other places like it don't exist. But drive thirty-five kilometres from the city and there it is.

Any former policy wonk, even one like me with an aversion to the inanities of managerialism, could easily reel off a long list of things that might help solve Doveton's problems, if we really cared enough about them. I'd start more concretely (and no doubt more naively) than the economic development experts: get the government to subsidise a company to build a big factory, and demand that it gives unskilled and semi-skilled jobs to the unemployed people and school leavers from Doveton; spend millions repainting houses, replacing gutters, planting trees and resealing the footpaths to brighten the place up as part of a comprehensive neighbourhood regeneration project; offer young families with jobs incentives to move in and add some energy and affluence to the place; perhaps even bus the high-school kids to Melbourne Grammar.

In other words, I'm saying that if people are jobless, give them jobs; if their houses are eyesores, beautify them and remove the stigma; if new blood is needed, bring it in; if an education will solve everything, give them the best one money can buy.

As Panda tells me, small steps have been taken in these directions, but perhaps nowhere near enough. There is a community farm, where my sisters' grandchildren regularly have their birthday parties, and where there is an annual agricultural show. An impressive wetland wildlife sanctuary, built using local unemployed labour, now adjoins it. Panda tells me that my old street is being populated by a new generation, including refugees from countries like Afghanistan who couldn't be prouder of their new homes. They too are spawning new small businesses. Keeping this going will cost, and plenty, but how much have we spent in the last thirty years, through our welfare system and our mental health system and our prison system, paying for failure? These people are worth it! (And how much, for that matter, have we subsidised property prices through negative gearing and the capital gains tax discount?)

Positive proposals like mine are the sorts of things we used to do. It's how Doveton was created in the first place, and how it gave me and my friends happy childhoods and a decent start in life, and our parents a standard of living they could get nowhere else. And it's when we stopped doing these things and put our misplaced faith in the hands of the creative destroyers that it all began to fall apart.

But these ideas are beyond our policymakers today, and there's little point in offering them up for discussion. If we are to give new life to places like Doveton, we must first change the way we think – and this goes especially for the Labor Party, whose heartlands (real *places of the heart*) suburbs like Doveton once were. Our imaginations have been stolen from us. We need to lift our minds beyond the ideas of the now stale revolution of thirty years ago, and beyond the narrowing philosophy of economic reform, with its enervating cult of managerialism and its mono-maniacal pursuit of productivity. We need to think wider and deeper, and see things in moral terms once again. We need to build on the past, not wipe it out. We need to re-capture, if we can, the romantic, animating, Promethean fire of the imagination that once led us to try to create a country ruled by the idea of decency, and which gave people in places like Doveton things almost impossible to conceive of today: affluence, success, happiness, perhaps even just a job, a home and somebody to love.

Most of all, we need once again to care about places like Doveton – to *really* care, the way we once did – because if we don't, nothing will ever change.

Ask yourself: do you care? Really care? Do you?

ACKNOWLEDGMENTS

There are indeed good people who care about Doveton and the manufacturing industries that once supported it. While I was writing this book, so many people stepped forward, eager to help. It's their story too, after all.

This includes family members: Audrey Glover, Fred Miles, Dawn Sutherland, Pamela Slivarich, Ena Gilliland, Anna Gregory and Jackie Gregory. And it includes friends: John Pandazopoulos (who helped me rediscover much, and has devoted his life to serving the people of Doveton), Jim McVicar (you never had a best friend like you did when you were twelve), Michael Hendricks, David Rowlands, Grant Coulter, Nick Zomer, John Wylie, Chris Cullin, Neil Moles, John Miles, Henry Torres and George Marin. I also want to acknowledge the many former employees of Heinz who spoke to me at the factory's fifteen-year reunion, especially my sister's friends from the packing line: Cheryl, Anne, Lorene, Louise, Shane and Wayne.

Thanks also to the former and present senior managers and executives of General Motors Holden who spoke to me – Ian McCleave, Russel Nainie, Barry Crees and Geoff Mowthorpe – as well as to Mounir Kiwan of the Federation of Automotive Parts Manufacturers, who put me in touch with them. And to municipal economic development officers Paula Brennan (of the City of Dandenong) and Tom Szolt (of the City of Casey). Adrian Boden of the South East Melbourne Manufacturer's Alliance gave me the background on industry in the Dandenong region. The acting principal of Doveton College, Greg McMahon, and his staff and students spent precious time telling me about their gutsy efforts on behalf of their local community. Magistrate Pauline Spencer from the Dandenong Court allowed me access to her busy court, and shared many important insights about the dire social problems experienced by many local residents. Tim Kennedy, National Secretary of the National Union of Workers – one of the brightest union officials in Australia – gave me the perspective on change from warehousing workers. Adjunct Professor Lisa Heap of the Australian Catholic University and the Australian Institute of Employment Rights discussed with me similar issues of manufacturing unemployment elsewhere in Australia and Detroit. The social researcher Tony Vinson pointed me to places similar to Doveton. Deputy Labor

Party leader Anthony Albanese, who grew up in a place not unlike Doveton, gave me insights into working-class life in other parts of Australia.

Zoe McKenzie provided her beach house as the perfect writer's retreat where the final draft was completed. It is always highly appreciated.

The team at my think tank, Per Capita, have been supportive and inspiring. As always, I salute them, especially Emily, David and Anthony, whose ideas and intellectual ambition have influenced this book enormously.

My editor from Black Inc., Julian Welch, has done a terrific job removing the rhetorical excesses to which this speechwriter is inclined, and in panelbeating the manuscript into its final shape. I thank Julian and his colleague Chris Feik for commissioning the book.

Finally, I thank Fiona, Toby and Teddy for cutting me the slack without which a husband or parent could never write anything.

NOTES

The epigraph is from the ode 'Intimations of Immortality from Recollections of Early Childhood' by William Wordsworth.

INTRODUCTION
The quote from Heilbroner is from *The Worldly Philosophers: The Lives, Times, and Ideas of the Great Economic Thinkers* by Robert L. Heilbroner (Simon & Schuster, 1980), p. 311.

CHAPTER 1
Parts of the story of my crescent and my father's life story were told in the *Age* and other Fairfax newspapers on 8 February 2014; the piece was reprinted in *The Best Australian Essays 2014*, edited by Robert Manne (Black Inc., 2014).

CHAPTER 2
The epigraph is from Percy Bysshe Shelley's 'Ode to a Skylark'.

My tomato-stained copy of *The Grundrisse* is *Marx's Grundrisse*, edited by David McClellan (Paladin, 1973). The sections on creative destruction are at pp. 100–101 and pp. 111–112.

The NATSEM figures are from *Prices These Days: The Cost of Living in Australia*, NATSEM 2012, p. 21.

Unemployment figures for Doveton and Dandenong come from
Small Area Labour Markets, December Quarter 2014,
Department of Employment, Commonwealth of Australia.

Historical income and inequality statistics about Doveton and
workforce totals for the Big Three come from two previous
studies of Doveton – *An Australian Newtown: Life and Leadership
in a New Housing Suburb* by Lois Bryson & Faith Thompson
(Penguin, 1972) and *Social Change, Suburban Lives: An
Australian Newtown, 1960s to 1990s*, by Lois Bryson & Ian Winter
(Allen & Unwin, 1999) – and from Australian Census QuickStats
for postcode 2011.

CHAPTER 3
The epigraph is from 'Ozymandias' by Shelley's friend Horace Smith.

The closing poetic paraphrase is from Shelley's version of
'Ozymandias'.

CHAPTER 4
The epigraph is from Shelley's 'Ode to the West Wind'.

The Making of the English Working Class by E. P. Thompson was
published by Gollancz in 1963. I have used the Penguin 1982
edition. My quotations are from the Preface and Chapter 6.

My discussion on productivity owes something to my reading of
the many columns on the subject by the *Age*'s economics
columnist Ross Gittins, although the conclusions are my own.

The insights on America come from *The Unwinding: Thirty Years
of American Decline* by George Packer (Faber & Faber, 2013).

CHAPTER 5
The epigraph is from George Orwell's *Nineteen Eighty-Four*.

The quote from Friedrich Engels comes from *The Frock-Coated
Communist: The Revolutionary Life of Friedrich Engels* by Tristram
Hunt (Allen Lane, 2009), p. 107.

CONCLUSION
The epigraph is from a letter from Mary Wollstonecraft to Gilbert
Imlay, taken from *Footsteps: Adventures of a Romantic Biographer*,
by Richard Holmes (Harper Perennial, 2005), p. 27.

BATTLERS & BILLIONAIRES
THE STORY OF INEQUALITY IN AUSTRALIA
Andrew Leigh

REDBACK 1

'Required reading for every Australian who seriously cares about the fair go enduring.'
—Peter FitzSimons

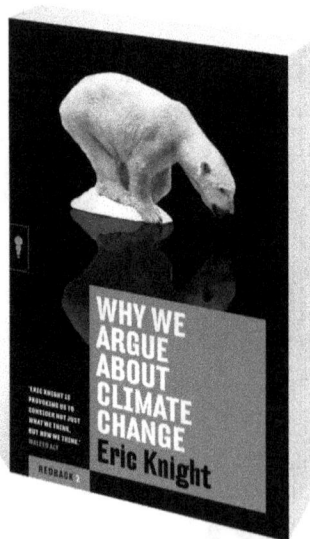

WHY WE ARGUE ABOUT CLIMATE CHANGE
Eric Knight

'ERIC KNIGHT IS PROVOKING US TO CONSIDER NOT JUST WHAT WE THINK, BUT HOW WE THINK.'
WALEED ALY

REDBACK

'Eric Knight is provoking us to consider not just what we think, but how we think.'
—Waleed Aly

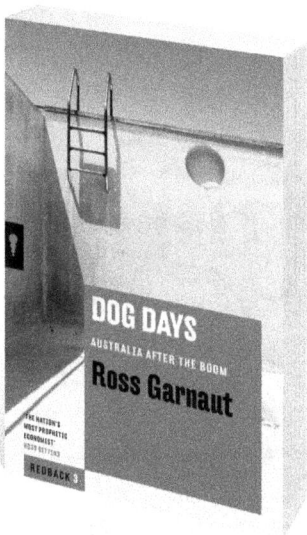

CRIME & PUNISHMENT

OFFENDERS AND VICTIMS
IN A BROKEN JUSTICE SYSTEM

Russell Marks

REDBACK S

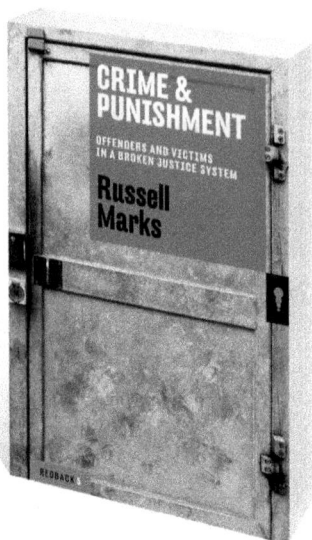

'A reflective, well-argued
book ... what makes it even
more compelling is Marks
also offers suggestions on a
different (better) system of
crime and punishment.'
—*Sydney Morning Herald*

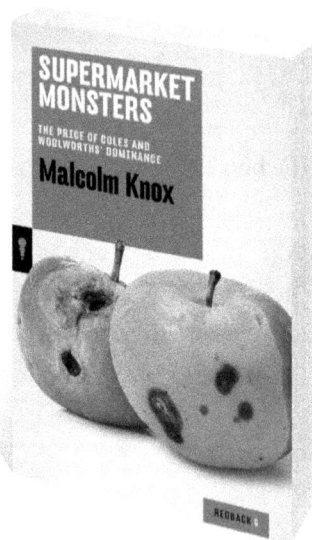

SUPERMARKET MONSTERS

THE PRICE OF COLES AND
WOOLWORTHS' DOMINANCE

Malcolm Knox

REDBACK S

Supermarket Monsters
shines a light on Coles and
Woolworths, Australia's twin
mega-retailers, exploring
how they have built and
exploited their market
power. What does their
dominance mean for
suppliers? And is it good
for consumers?